Sewing
Dolls' Clothes

Sewing
Dolls' Clothes

27 PROJECTS TO MAKE IN 1:12 SCALE

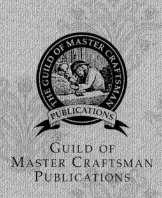

GUILD OF
MASTER CRAFTSMAN
PUBLICATIONS

First published 2007 by

GUILD OF MASTER CRAFTSMAN PUBLICATIONS LTD
Castle Place, 166 High Street,
Lewes, East Sussex BN7 1XU

All photographs by Anthony Bailey, except on page 10 by Robin Harmsworth
and pages 18, 30, 32, 33 by Nick Nickholson

All illustrations by Janet Harmsworth/Rob Wheele except
for page 31 by Doug Harding and page 99 by Sue Johnson/Rob Wheele

Production Manager: Jim Bulley
Managing Editor: Gerrie Purcell
Editor: Virginia Brehaut
Managing Art Editor: Gilda Pacitti

Set in Brandyscript and Stymie

Colour origination by Altaimage
Printed and bound in
China by Sino Publishing

Foreword

Although the majority of us do not make the actual dolls that live in our dolls' houses, we can have control over what they wear by dressing the figures that we buy. Dressing dolls' house dolls can be quite a challenge, with the pattern pieces being so small, but that sense of achievement when our dolls are fully clothed is so rewarding it is worth persevering.

Choosing fabrics and trims to turn into miniature outfits is an enjoyable part of the hobby. Such small amounts are required that it is easy to pick up fabulous silks and cottons that would be beyond the full-size clothing budget. You can also make use of real garments that have become too worn for your wardrobe. As long as any pattern is in a suitably small scale and the fabric not too thick you can give your fashion favourites a new lease of life in your dolls' house. Old cloth also has a patina all of its own and, if you can find it, vintage lace is a real asset to the period costume. Unlike real clothes, miniature ones do not have to be removable and can be sewn (or sometimes even glued) together with no tricky hooks, zips or buttonholes.

These clothing patterns were originally commissioned for *The Dolls' House Magazine*, but it is wonderful to see them combined into this one useful volume. The women who designed the patterns are accomplished seamstresses when it comes to dressing miniature dolls. Their instructions make the whole process seem effortless. The text is clearly laid out with the 1:12 scale patterns pieces ready for you to trace off for immediate use.

With such expertise to guide you, you'll be able to create fashionable figures for a wide variety of historical periods and settings. I'm sure that you'll love the results.

Christiane Berridge,
Editor, *The Dolls' House Magazine*

Pattern Notes

All patterns are reproduced 100% size.

A seam allowance of ⅛in (3mm) has been allowed on the patterns, unless otherwise stated.

Contents

Fashionable Ladies

Dressing for Work

In the Country

Special Occasions

Fancy Dress

Fashionable Ladies

This pattern is based on the year 1483, the time of the Princes in the Tower, not long before the battle of Bosworth where Richard III was defeated and Henry Tudor claimed the throne. This brought an end to the House of York and began the Tudor period.

Materials

Female doll with
 dropped shoulders
Cotton fabric for dress
Fur trim or decorative
 braid
White/cream cotton for
 underwear
Lace edging
Paint for shoes
Tacky glue
Viscose wigging
Picot braid
1½in (36mm) wide
 gauze ribbon
Bondaweb
Hairspray
No-hole beads and
 crystals (optional)
Water-based sealer
 (optional)

Gothic Gown

WEALTHY WOMEN OF THE MIDDLE AGES COULD BE IDENTIFIED BY THEIR FLOWING GOWNS IN BRIGHT COLOURS AND ELABORATE HEADWEAR.

Preparation

Trace pattern pieces and check the sizes against your doll. Then make any necessary adjustments. To make sure of the fit and construction make up pattern in kitchen paper first. When happy with the pattern pieces lay them out on the relevant fabric, remembering to reverse them where necessary.

Place on fold

Kirtle
Cut 1

Gown side
Cut 2

Straight of grain

Straight of grain

Gown back
Cut 2

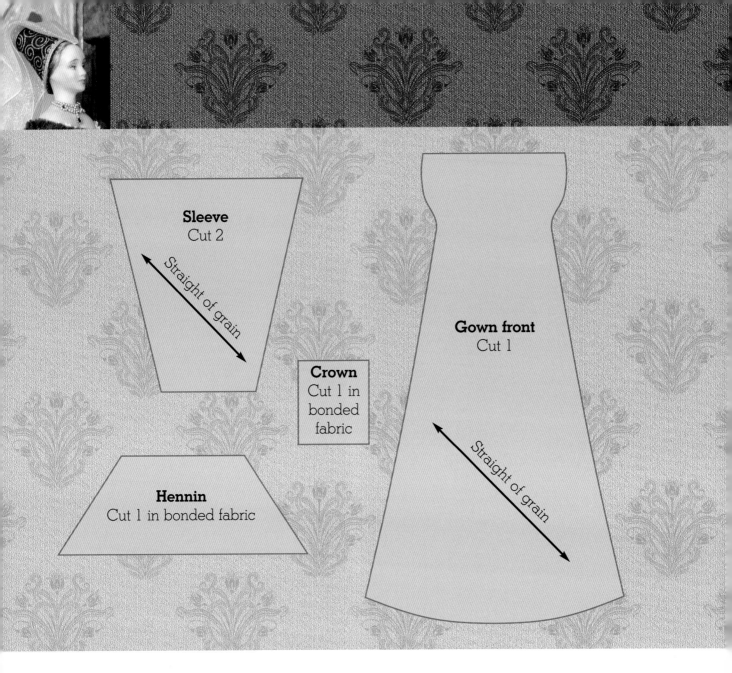

Draw round patterns with tailor's chalk or erasable fabric pen. Then run a thin beading of tacky glue along the pattern lines and let dry to stop the fabric from fraying. Cut out pattern pieces.

Paint shoes in desired colour, sealing with a coat of varnish if acrylics are used.

Kirtle

The kirtle was an undergarment – an early form of petticoat – and the only one worn.

1 Turn up the hem and add lace edging. Stitch the centre back seam.

2 Run a gathering stitch around the top. Fit onto doll under the bust; pull up the gathering thread, arranging the gathers evenly.

3 Glue a length of lace around the top of the doll's bust and shoulders. This is the top of the kirtle, just showing above the gown.

Hennin (hat)

This cone-shaped hat was stylish for women of the nobility at the time. The fashion was for a high hairline, and for the hairline and eyebrows to be plucked. Wig your doll with the hair pulled back off the face.

1 Lap angled side over the other and glue (achieving a cone shape) and leave to dry.

2 Run a bead of glue around the smaller hole. Place crown piece on top and leave to dry.

3 When thoroughly dry, trim around the shape of the top as close as you can.

4 Trim the top and bottom of the cone with picot braid.

5 Twist your ribbon in the centre to form a pointy cone shape. Secure the shape with a stitch or glue.

6 Stick the ribbon onto the top of the hennin, with the point jutting out over the doll's forehead. Leave to dry.

The Gown

This is made with the skirt and bodice all in one, and consists of five panels sewn together.

1 Stitch front to side panels A–B, C–D.

2 Stitch the side panels to the back panels E–F, and G–H.

3 Stitch the centre back seam I–J, starting down from the top as marked on the pattern. Press all the seams. Turn up or glue the hem.

4 Fit the gown onto the doll, glue top of gown onto the doll's bust. Any gap between the gown and the top of the kirtle will be covered with fur trim later.

Gown Sleeves

1 With the right sides together stitch the underarm seam and press. Turn the sleeve the right sides out.

2 Run a gathering thread around the top of the sleeve. Fit the sleeve onto doll; pull up gathering thread until a good fit is achieved.

3 Turn under the raw edge and stitch the sleeve in place, stitching into lace kirtle on the shoulder.

Trimming

Trim the top of the bodice, hemline and cuffs with a trim of your choice (I used faux fur). Add any jewellery that you wish. I drew my necklace design onto the doll lightly in pencil, and added the beads one by one building up the design as I went. I secured the beads with a coat of water-based sealer.

The Regency period was
a short time at the end
of the 18th century and the
start of the 19th century.
Gone were the wide
Georgian-style dresses and
large hairstyles. Soft muslin
gowns in pale colours and
muted patterns were
designed in the Roman/
Greek Classical style.
The very fashionable and
daring ladies of the time
would wear their sheer
skirts dampened down so
that they would cling to
their bodies, wearing only
pink tights underneath.
This seems only to have
been reserved for those
few ladies blessed with
good figures, most others
would have resorted to
whalebone stays to achieve
the slim-line look.

Materials

Female doll with full
    arms
Fine white cotton for
    petticoat
Fine patterned fabric
    for dress
Lace
Ribbon

Regency Lady

THIS REGENCY LADY IS READY FOR A STROLL IN THE
GARDEN OR ACROSS THE FIELDS ON A SUMMER'S DAY
IN HER MUSLIN GOWN AND HER PARASOL TO PROTECT
HER FACE FROM THE SUN.

Petticoat
Cut 1

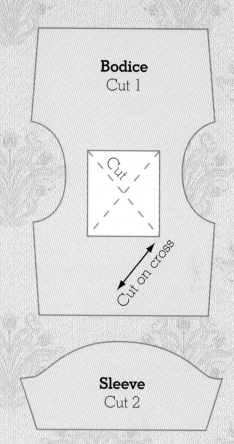

Bodice
Cut 1

Cut

Cut on cross

Sleeve
Cut 2

Skirt
Cut 1 on fold of fabric

Place on fold

Preparation

Trace pattern pieces and check for size against your doll. Make any necessary adjustments. To make sure of fit or construction, make the pattern up in kitchen paper first. Once happy with your pattern pieces, lay them out on the relevant fabric, remember to reverse pattern pieces where necessary. Draw round pattern with either tailor's chalk or erasable fabric pen. Run a thin beading of tacky glue along pattern lines (to prevent fabric fraying) and allow to dry before cutting out. Paint shoes white using either enamel or acrylic paint. If acrylic paint is used then a coat of varnish will also be required.

Petticoat

1 Turn up hem and attach lace to hem.

2 Stitch the centre back seam and press it open.

3 Run a gathering thread around the waist of petticoat. Fit onto your doll, pulling up gathering thread and secure. Arrange the folds evenly around the waist.

Dress

1 Turn up hem on the skirt and glue or stitch in place.

2 Run a gathering thread around top of skirt. Run a beading of glue around doll, just under the bust line.

3 Fit skirt onto doll, ensuring that the gathered edge is well over the glue. Pull up gathering thread and secure.

4 Cut neck opening on the bodice as indicated on the pattern.

5 Fold in each of the four triangles, to make a neat, square neckline. Snip the points off the triangles and glue the remainder of the flaps down.

6 Stitch one side seam and press. Fit the bodice onto your doll. Fold under the seam allowance on the front bodice and glue or stitch seam in place.

7 Fold under raw edge on the bottom of bodice and slip stitch bodice to top of skirt.

8 Turn under a tiny seam on the bottom of both sleeves.

9 Sew underarm seam of both sleeves and press.

10 Run a gathering stitch around the top of both sleeves.

11 Fit sleeve onto doll and pull up gathering thread until a good fit is achieved.

12 Turn in raw edge around top of sleeve and slipstitch sleeve to bodice.

13 Run another gathering stitch around bottom of sleeve, pull up tight to create a puffed sleeve, then repeat for the other sleeve.

14 Trim the dress with a ribbon tie under the bust, ribbon around the neckline and ribbon bows on each sleeve.

Wigging

Wig your doll in either of the following Regency styles:

Classical upswept hair, dressed on the crown of the head with lots of wispy tendrils around the forehead.

Masses of short curls all over the head with a ribbon worn like an Alice band.

This costume reflects the style of 1870, when the previous fullness of skirts had moved to the rear, usually supported by a bustle. Hair was worn high in ringlets or a knot with a small hat or veil perched on top.

Materials

Female doll
White cotton lawn for
   bloomers, petticoat
   and bustle
Silk for dress, skirt and
   sleeves
Contrasting silk for
   dress bodice and
   apron
Double picot braid for
   shoes
Black acrylic paint for
   shoes
Acrylic varnish for shoes
Medium weight card
   for hat
⁹⁄₃₂in (7mm), ⁵⁄₃₂in (4mm)
   and ⁵⁄₆₄in (2mm) silk
   ribbon for sash and
   parasol
Cocktail stick for parasol
Assorted lace, braid and
   feathers for hat

Dickensian Costume

THIS LADY IS PERFECTLY DRESSED FOR BROWSING AROUND TOWN IN BOOKSHOPS, PERHAPS ENQUIRING AFTER THE LATEST DICKENS SERIALIZATION.

Preparation

The pattern pieces show the sewing line. When cutting out allow for a seam allowance. Before cutting the pattern out in fabric, make up in kitchen paper and use to make any adjustments necessary for the pattern to fit your doll.

Boots

Before dressing the doll, paint the feet, and 1in (25mm) of the leg with black acrylic paint and seal with gloss acrylic varnish. To give the effect of a laced boot, glue double picot braid down the front of the painted boot.

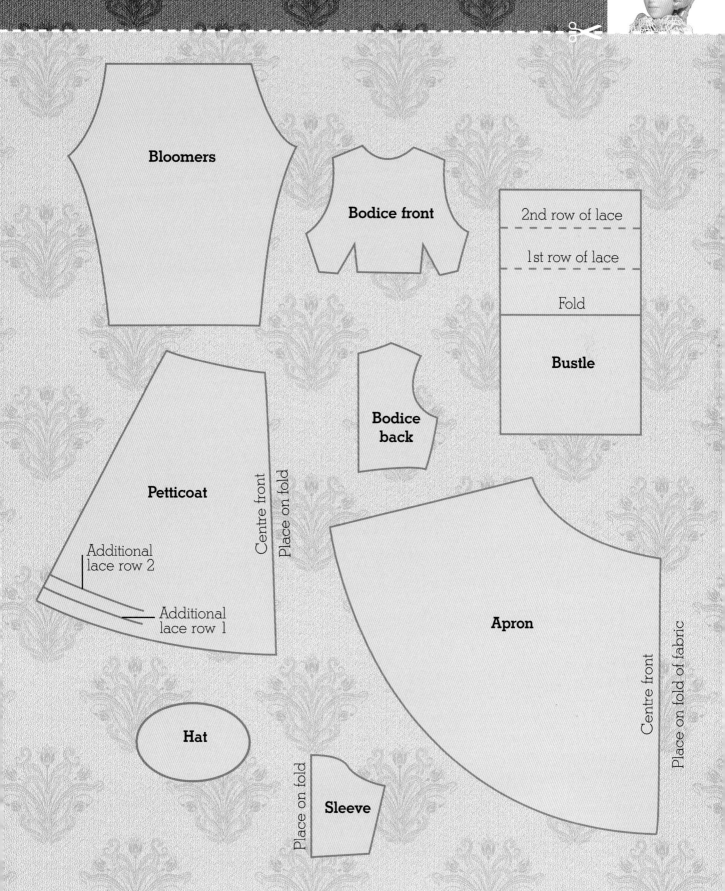

Bloomers

Bodice front

2nd row of lace

1st row of lace

Fold

Bustle

Petticoat

Centre front

Place on fold

Bodice back

Additional lace row 2

Additional lace row 1

Apron

Centre front

Place on fold of fabric

Hat

Place on fold

Sleeve

Bloomers

1 Cut two pattern pieces from fine, white cotton lawn.

2 Trim the bottom edge of the drawers with $\frac{1}{2}$in (12mm) lace.

3 Stitch front and back seams, and then centre leg seams.

4 Run a gathering thread around the waist edge.

5 Fit onto the doll, taking all the gathers to the back of the waist.

6 Stitch to the body of the doll, just below the waist.

7 Attach a bow, made from $\frac{5}{64}$in (2mm) wide white silk ribbon.

Petticoat

Make the petticoat from fine, white cotton lawn.

1 Gather sufficient $\frac{1}{2}$in (12mm) wide white cotton lace to trim the bottom edge of the petticoat.

2 Stitch the gathered lace to the hem of the petticoat.

3 For additional volume to the back of the petticoat add a further two rows of gathered lace as shown on the pattern.

4 Run a gathering thread around the waist edge and fit onto the doll, taking all the gathers to the back of the waist.

5 Stitch to the body of the doll, just below the waist.

Bustle

Make the bustle from fine, white cotton lawn.

1 Cut one of the bustle base.

2 With right side together, fold the base in half, and stitch the side seams.

3 Turn right side out.

4 Gather $\frac{1}{2}$in (12mm) wide white cotton lace very tightly and stitch in place – see pattern. Repeat this again.

5 Turn in raw edges at top of bustle, and slipstitch closed.

6 Sew onto doll at the back of the waist, above the petticoat.

Dress Skirt

This is made from one piece of silk. Check the length of the skirt before pleating, and always finish the skirt before pleating by sewing a simple hem. Pleat sufficient silk to fill the whole board. It is easier to pleat silk that is damp. When the pleating is complete, do not

remove the silk from the pleater until it is completely dry (leave it in the pleater overnight if necessary).

1 Stitch the back seam of the skirt.

2 Run a gathering thread around the top of the skirt.

3 Fit the skirt onto the doll, taking all the excess fullness to the back of the doll to help form the bustle shape.

4 Stitch the skirt to the doll at the waist.

Dress Bodice

Use a contrasting silk for the dress bodice, sleeves and apron. A hairline striped silk works well.

1 Sew the front bodice darts.

2 Stitch the shoulder and side seams.

3 Fit onto the doll, ensuring that the bodice is a snug fit.

4 Slip stitch the back seam.

5 Gather some $\frac{1}{2}$in (12mm) lace and sew into place around the neck edge of the bodice.

Dress Sleeves

1 Stitch the underarm seams.

2 Run a gathering thread along the top of the sleeve and fit onto the doll.

3 Pull up the gathering thread at the top of the sleeve so that it fits neatly. Sew into place.

4 Trim the wrist edge of the sleeve with $\frac{1}{2}$in (12mm) gathered lace, and narrow silk ribbon. Finish with a bow made from silk ribbon.

5 Trim the shoulder edge of the sleeves with bows made from $\frac{5}{32}$in (4mm) silk ribbon.

Apron

1 Cut the apron in contrasting silk, and silk for lining.

2 With the right sides together, sew the bottom and sides together, but leave the top open.

3 Clip the curves; turn through to the right side, and press.

4 Trim the edges of the bustle with pleated silk, lace and gathered or ruched $\frac{5}{32}$in (4mm) silk ribbon.

5 Join the back seams of the apron with a gathering thread.

6 Fit onto doll, and draw any excess fullness to the back of the waist.

7 Draw up the gathering thread to $1\frac{1}{2}$in (38mm). Secure the thread. Sew into place.

8 Make a sash to go around the waist using $\frac{9}{32}$in (7mm) silk ribbon, and secure this at the back of the waist.

9 Gather, or ruffle, sufficient $\frac{9}{32}$in (7mm) silk ribbon to make a ruffle of enough length to cover the back seam of the apron. It is easier to glue, rather than sew, this into place.

Hat

1 Cut out the pattern piece in medium weight card.

2 Cover with silk fabric.

3 Trim with pleated fabric, lace, braid and feathers.

Parasol

1 Cover a wooden cocktail stick with $\frac{9}{32}$in (7mm) wide silk ribbon. Trim with ruffled $\frac{5}{32}$in (4mm) silk ribbon.

2 Make a handle by gluing a $\frac{5}{64}$in (2mm) silk ribbon loop to the top of the parasol. Put the loop over the dolls' wrist.

This Victorian lady is straight out of the middle of a 19th-century fashion plate. A stiffened petticoat supports her crinoline dress. Capes were in vogue, as they were very practical to wear over wide skirts. Bonnets were still popular, but by this time the width of the brim was decreasing so that a lady's profile could be seen.

Materials

Female doll in
   pantaloons
Cotton fabric for dress
White cotton for
   petticoat
Thin velvet or velour
   for cape
Faux fur trim
Lace edging
Braid/ trim for dress
   and hat
Paint for shoes
Tacky glue
Bondaweb
Viscose wigging
Hairspray
(See page 126 for
suppliers of miniature
ice skate blades.)

Victorian Skater

THIS ENCHANTING COSTUME IS PERFECT FOR A CRISP, ICY, WINTER'S DAY. IT COULD ALSO BE USED FOR A CAROL SINGER OR A WINTER SHOPPING OUTFIT.

Preparation

Trace pattern pieces and check the sizes against your doll. Make any necessary adjustments. To make sure of the fit, make up pattern in kitchen paper first.

When happy with the pattern pieces lay them out on the relevant fabric, remembering to reverse them as necessary. Draw round patterns with

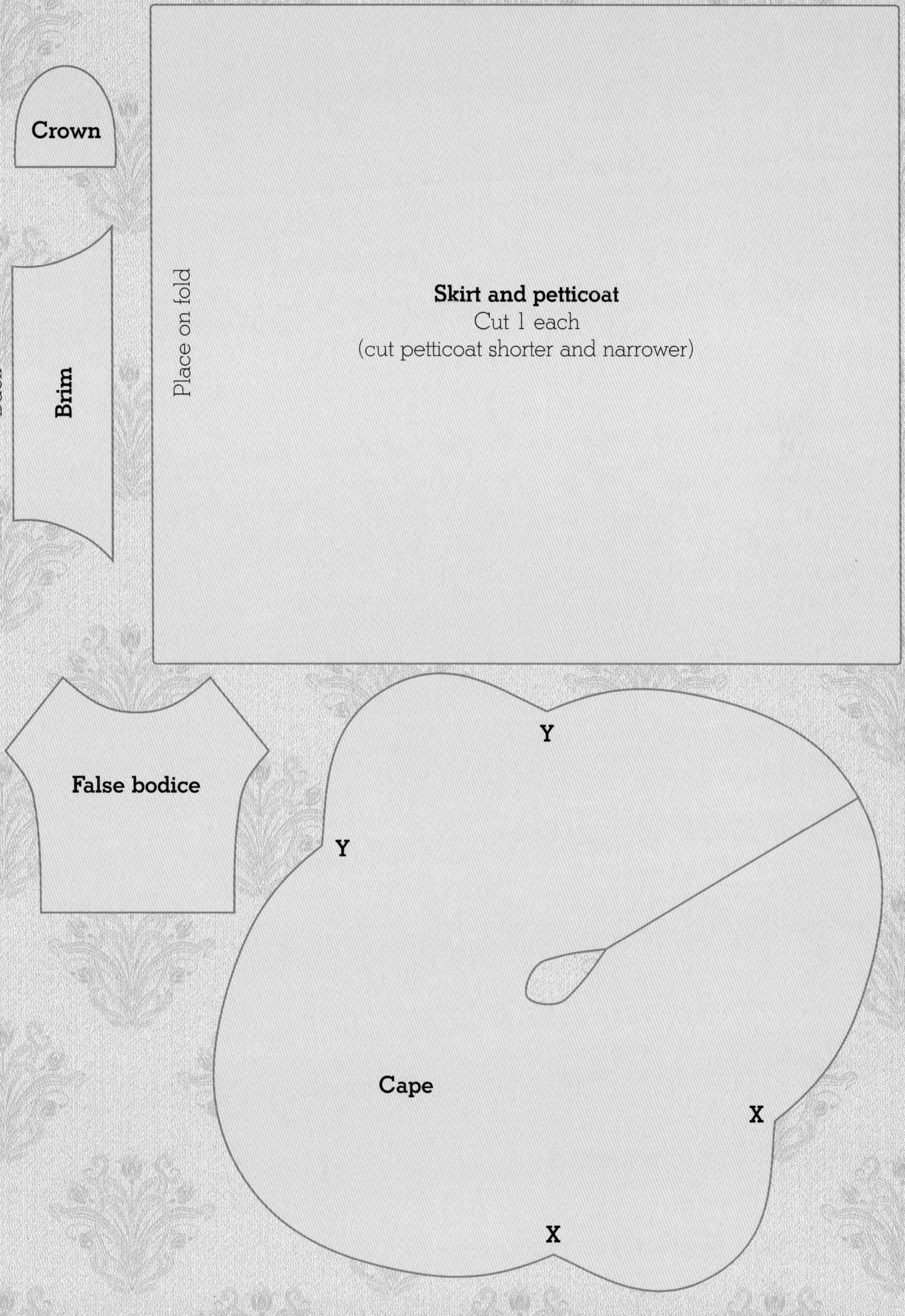

Crown

Back

Brim

Place on fold

Skirt and petticoat
Cut 1 each
(cut petticoat shorter and narrower)

False bodice

Y

Y

Cape

X

X

tailor's chalk or erasable fabric pen. Then run a thin beading of tacky glue along the pattern lines and let dry to stop the fabric from fraying. Cut out pattern pieces. Paint shoes in your desired colour, sealing with a coat of varnish if acrylics are used.

Skirt

1 Turn up hem and stitch.

2 Stitch the centre back seam, again using a French seam for a neater finish.

3 Run a gathering thread around the waist, fit onto doll, pull up gathers and arrange the folds evenly around the doll's waist.

False Bodice Front

1 Glue the bodice to the doll's chest. Pinch in and glue the bust darts if needed.

2 Turn under a raw edge at waist for a neat finish.

3 Add a little lace to the neck and front if desired.

Petticoat

1 Turn up and stitch the hem. Attach lace if desired.

2 Stitch centre back seam using a French seam for a neater finish.

3 Run a gathering thread around the doll's waist, fit the skirt onto the doll, pull up the gathers arranging them evenly around the waist.

4 Spray the whole of the petticoat with hairspray and allow to dry. Several applications may be required to achieve a stiff petticoat to support the crinoline skirt.

Sleeve and Cape

1 Add a false cuff around the doll's wrist so that a little of it shows below the cape.

2 Treat the raw edge of the cape with glue to prevent fraying.

3 Glue faux fur trim around the edge, neck and front of cape.

4 Fit cape onto the doll.

5 Stab stitch the sleeves together where marked.

6 Slipstitch the front together.

Wigging

This doll is wigged in a simple style with a front parting. Her hat covers her hairstyle.

Bonnet

1 Cut the two pattern pieces out of bonded fabric. If you don't have any Bondaweb or similar to hand, glue some fabric to both sides of a thin piece of card and cut your pattern pieces from that.

2 Apply a thin beading of glue around the arch of the crown piece.

3 Glue the back of the brim to the crown. I use an old mascara tube as a block to help support the pieces while they bond. Allow to dry (the hat should resemble half an American mailbox).

4 Trim all the edges and around the crown with picot braid.

5 Finish hat off by adding ribbons and trimmings of your choice. I used ribbons and paper flowers.

Edwardian fashion (circa 1901–1910) saw the beginnings of a narrower skirt style which skimmed the hips and then widened at the hemline. The style was pretty and fussy, with dainty bags and wide, lavish hats adorned with feathers and ribbon.

Materials

Female doll
White silk
1¾in (44mm) wide
    cotton lace
Thin cotton lace
9⁄32in (7mm) wide white
    silk ribbon
Bunka
Picot edging
Feathers
Silk flowers
Bondaweb
Dylon fabric pen
Cocktail stick
Small pearly bead

Edwardian Chic

THIS STYLISH CHARACTER COULD HAVE STEPPED OUT OF THE ASCOT SCENE IN THE FILM *MY FAIR LADY*. SHE IS CERTAINLY DRESSED TO MINGLE WITH HIGH SOCIETY.

Sleeve
Cut 2

Front
Cut 2

Back
Cut 2

Hat
Cut in bonded fabric

Parasol
Cut 1

Preparation

Trace pattern pieces and check for size against your doll. Make any necessary adjustments. To make sure of fit make the pattern up in kitchen paper first. Once happy with your pattern pieces lay them out on the relevant fabric, reversing pattern pieces where necessary. Draw round pattern with either tailor's chalk or erasable fabric pen. Run a thin beading of tacky glue along pattern lines and allow to dry before cutting out. Paint shoes or boots using either enamel or acrylic paints. If acrylics are used a coat of varnish will be needed to seal the paint.

Dress

1 Stitch back seam of the dress to the mark, and press the seam open.

2 Stitch the front seams together, clip the curve and press the seam open.

3 Stitch the side seams, clip the curves and press the seam open.

4 Stitch both shoulder seams and press.

5 Turn up the hem.

6 Fit the dress onto your doll and slipstitch back seam.

Dress Sleeves

1 Turn under the raw edge along the bottom of each sleeve.

2 Stitch the underarm seam and press. Turn the sleeves right side out.

3 Run a gathering thread around the top of each sleeve and fit the sleeve on to the doll. Pull up the threads until a good fit is achieved.

4 Turn under the raw edge and slipstitch the sleeve in place.

Under Frill

1 Cut a strip 7in (177mm) by 1¾in (44mm) in the same fabric as the dress.

2 Turn up a hem along one long edge.

3 Stitch the back seam and then press.

4 Run a gathering thread along the top of the frill.

5 Pull up the frill to fit the bottom of the dress then stitch or glue it in place under the hem.

Lace Frill

1 Pleat a length of 1¾in (44mm) wide lace.

2 Stitch or glue the back seam together.

3 Stitch the frill around the hemline on top of the dress.

4 Neaten around the top of the lace with a strip of $^9/_{32}$in (7mm) wide ribbon.

Dress Trimmings

1 Trim the neckline with a strip of fine lace.

2 Trim cuff of sleeves with gathered lace.

3 Trim the dress with strips of striped ribbon, a bow at the hemline and a large pussy-cat bow at the shoulder.

Parasol

1 Trim the curved edge with pleated lace and bunka.

2 Fold the parasol to form a cone shape and glue the seam closed. Leave a small hole at the bottom for the cocktail stick handel to poke through.

3 Run a gathering thread around the top of the parasol just under the lace trim.

4 Insert the cocktail stick into the parasol and out through the hole in the bottom.

5 Pull the gathering thread up around the stick. Add a drop of glue to secure.

6 Glue a small bead on top of the stick to make a handle.

7 Trim and decorate the parasol as you wish.

Dolly Bag

1 Take a small piece of lace and glue into a circle.

2 Run a gathering thread along the bottom (straight edge) and pull up tight and secure. Turn right side out.

3 Run a gathering thread along the top of the bag, just under the scalloped edge of lace.

4 Fill the bag with a little stuffing to give it shape.

5 Pull up the top gathers, add a handle and trimming.

Hat

1 Cut the hat from bonded silk, ie two pieces of silk bonded together using Bondaweb or a similar product.

2 Trim around the edge of the hat with black picot braiding.

3 Run a circle of gathering thread as indicated on the pattern.

4 Run up the gathering thread and secure to create the shape of the hat.

5 Lavishly trim the crown of the hat with ribbon bows, feathers and fabric flowers.

The 1920s saw a change to a less feminine and curvaceous shape of dress. The lines were simplified, supressing curves and hiding the waist. Cloche hats were worn with short hair and make-up was very precise with high, arched eyebrows and bright lips.

Materials

Acrylic paints
Fine paintbrush

For the customer:
White silk for drawers
White dupion silk for
  dress
Black and white chenille
  for trimming

For the maid:
White cotton for drawers
  and apron
Plain lace
Black silk for dress
3⁄8in (10mm) Broderie
  Anglaise for apron
5⁄64in (2mm) black silk
  ribbon for apron
9⁄32in (7mm) white silk
  ribbon for apron
Entredeaux edging for
  apron

Art Deco Style

THIS BASIC DRESS PATTERN IS VERY ADAPTABLE FOR 1920s CHARACTERS. THESE PAGES SHOW HOW A MAID AND HER CUSTOMER IN A CAFE SCENE CAN BE DRESSED USING IT.

Dressing the Dolls

The customer and the maid are dressed using the same pattern for the drawers and the dress. The drawers should closely fit the legs, and end at knee level. The simple dress pattern can be adapted to suit both characters.

Preparation

Before cutting out the pattern pieces in fabric, make a toile from kitchen paper, fit it on the doll and make any necessary adjustments.

You may need to paint the face of your doll to reflect the style of make-up of the 1920s. Use the finest paintbrush possible. The eyebrows need to be fine

Short sleeve edge

Sleeve

Long
sleeve edge

Drawers

Dress

Apron

A   **Apron lower
section**   B

C

and arched, with the eyelashes emphasized. Black acrylic paint applied with a dry brush gives a good effect. The lips need to be painted red, with the top lip having a bow shape. When the painting has been completed, it has to be sealed with a coat of matt acrylic varnish.

The legs of the dolls can be painted black, grey or left in a natural colour, but for the maid it is preferable that they be painted black. The shoes can be painted onto the doll in any suitable style. The legs and shoes should be sealed with varnish, but this can be either matt or gloss.

Basic Dresses

The object is to make a dress without a fitted waist, so you want to have as straight a line from the top to the bottom of the dress as is possible. When you are satisfied with the fit, cut the pattern out in iron-on boned cotton muslin interlining. Iron these pattern pieces onto the appropriate fabric. Use fray check to seal the neck and arm openings.

1 Stitch the shoulder seams, and press open.

2 Turn the hem of the dress, and either slipstitch or glue into place.

3 Fit the dress onto the doll, and either oversew or glue the back seams together.

4 Stitch the underarm seams of the sleeves, tuck in the raw edge at the armhole edge of the sleeve and fit onto the doll. Slipstitch or glue the sleeves onto the doll, ensuring the armholes of the dress are fully covered.

Customer

The drawers are made in white silk. The dress is made from white dupion silk using the full-length sleeve pattern, with the neck, cuffs and shoulder edging trimmed with some thick black chenille.

The earrings are made from flat-backed pin-head crystals. Her hat is ready made, but given an additional trim of thick white and black chenille in order to help it match the dress.

The Maid

Make the maid's drawers from white cotton edged with plain lace. Make her dress from black silk, but with a short version of the sleeves. Make a collar and sleeve cuffs from ⅜in (10mm) wide Broderie Anglaise.

1 The apron is made from fine white cotton. For the trimming, thread ⁵⁄₆₄in (2mm) black silk ribbon through white cotton entredeux.

2 Cut the white cotton edging from one side of the entredeux. Glue the other cotton edging to ⅜in (10mm) wide Broderie Anglaise.

3 Glue the entredeux and Broderie Anglaise to the two sides and hem of the bottom half of the apron. The top of the apron is trimmed with the Broderie Anglaise without the addition of the entredeux.

4 Take the trim from the waist edge of the apron top, over the shoulder, down to the same level as the front top of the apron skirt and glue into place. Do this for both sides of the apron.

5 Place a piece of ⁹⁄₃₂in (7mm) white silk ribbon along the front of the apron, at the lower edge of the apron top. Take the ribbon to the back of the dress, ensuring that it covers the edge of the Broderie Anglaise trim, and glue into place.

6 Make a bow of the same ribbon and glue in the centre back of the apron tie. Using ⁵⁄₆₄in (2mm) black silk ribbon, add a bow at the centre of the collar, and at each side of the apron just under the waist tie.

7 The cap is made in a similar way to the edging of the lower section of the apron, and is of sufficient length to go completely around the head of the doll. Glue into place and add a ⁵⁄₆₄in (2mm) black silk ribbon bow at the back of the cap.

Dressing for Work

The Georgian period was a time when aristocratic men wore very flamboyant and colourful styles. Their formal dress of coat, waistcoats and breeches followed the French style and were made from the best silk, brocade and velvet. Their shirts would be of the finest lawn with lace trimming their cuffs and neck cloths. Dandies of the time even painted their faces and wore high shoes with red heels. The servants would be clothed in a toned-down version of their employer's clothes. The style of the servant's uniform was to stay in fashion for many years.

Materials

Male doll
Blue silk cotton for coat
Cream silk for waistcoat
White cotton for shirt
Silk ribbon for cravat
White stretch cotton for
  stockings
Black leather for shoes
Silver beads for buttons
Lace for cuffs
Silver sewing thread
  or braid
White viscose for wig
Bondaweb
Shoe buckles
Black ribbon

Georgian Footman

THIS SMARTLY DRESSED FOOTMAN IS READY TO PERFORM HIS MANY DUTIES KEEPING HIM BUSY FROM DUSK TILL DAWN TO SERVE HIS EMPLOYER.

Preparation

Note that the shirt and waistcoat consist of just false fronts as this reduces the bulk under the coat.

Trace pattern pieces and check the sizes against your doll. Make any adjustments that are needed. To make sure of the fit and construction, make up the

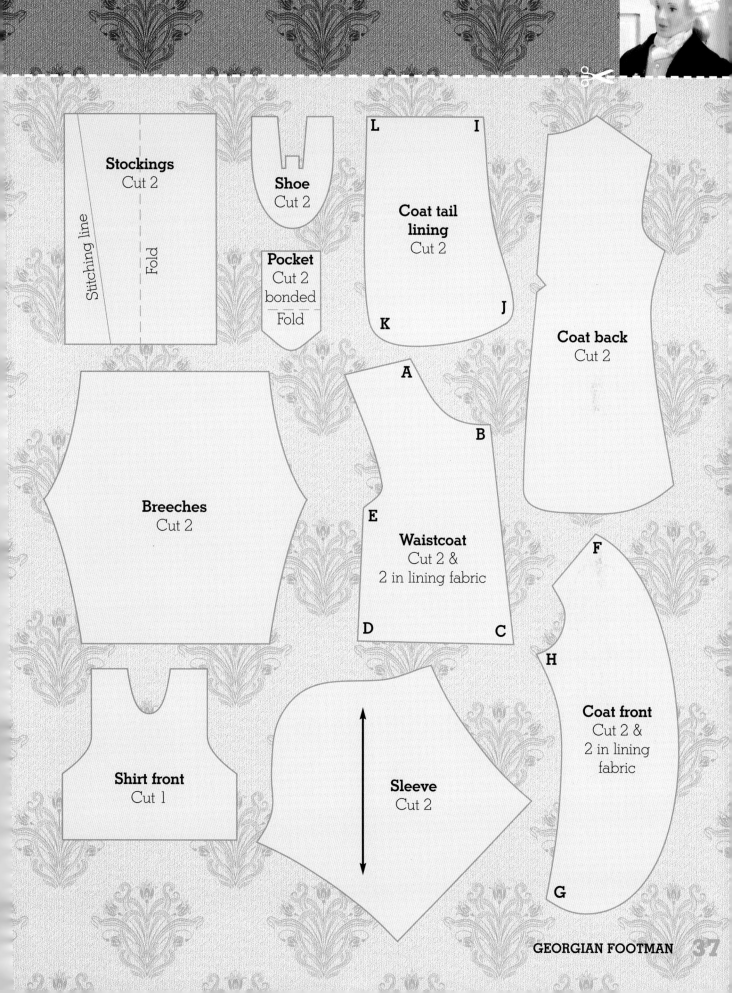

Stockings
Cut 2

Stitching line

Fold

Shoe
Cut 2

Pocket
Cut 2
bonded
Fold

L   I

Coat tail lining
Cut 2

K   J

Coat back
Cut 2

Breeches
Cut 2

A

B

E

Waistcoat
Cut 2 &
2 in lining fabric

D   C

F

H

Coat front
Cut 2 &
2 in lining fabric

G

Shirt front
Cut 1

Sleeve
Cut 2

pattern in kitchen paper first. When happy with the pattern pieces lay them out on the relevant fabric, remembering to reverse the pieces where necessary. Draw round patterns with either tailor's chalk or erasable fabric pen. Then run a thin beading of tacky glue along the pattern lines and allow to dry. This stops the fabric from fraying. Cut out pattern pieces.

Stockings

1 Fold each stocking piece in half with right sides facing together.

2 Stitch along the stitching lines. Trim seam close to stitching line. Turn right side out.

3 Fit onto doll, ensuring that the top of the foot is covered.

4 Secure the stockings with a little glue around the knee and the foot.

5 Trim away any excess under the foot.

Breeches

1 Stitch centre front and back seam, then clip the curve and press.

2 Check for length against your doll and turn up the hem. The breeches should finish just below the knee.

3 Stitch the inner leg seam. Clip seam at crotch. Turn right sides out and press.

4 Run a gathering thread around the waist. Fit onto doll, pulling up the thread at waist and secure.

5 Make a pleat on the outside of the leg at the knee to achieve a tight fit. Glue or stitch into place, adding a button for decoration.

Shirt and Cravat

1 Stick the shirt front onto your doll.

2 Make a cravat by wrapping a piece of silk ribbon around the dolls' neck a couple of times and tie at the front.

3 The long ties can be gathered to make a ruffle or left flat.

Waistcoat

1 Stitch front and front lining with right sides together from A–B–C–D–E.

2 Trim seams, clip around the neckline, turn right sides out and press.

3 Overlap the left-hand front over the right and stitch together. Sew buttons to front.

4 Fit waistcoat onto doll, lacing across the back and up to the shoulder tabs to secure (this won't show once the coat is on).

Shirt Cuffs

Gather a short length of lace and fit around each wrist as a ruffled cuff.

Coat

1 With right sides together, stitch coat front and lining from F–G–H. Trim seam, turn and press. Repeat for the other front.

2 With right sides together stitch tail lining to coat back I–J–K–L. Trim seam, turn right sides out and press.

3 Stitch centre back seam of coat to notch and press.

4 Stitch side seams and press.

5 Turn under the raw edge on the back of the neck.

6 Embroider decoration on the front of the coat using metallic thread (or use braid). Add bead buttons.

7 Bondaweb two pieces of coat fabric together and cut two pockets. Fold along the fold line shown on the pattern.

8 Decorate pocket flaps and glue pockets in place. Fit coat onto doll.

Coat Sleeves

1 Turn up a hem on each sleeve.

2 With right sides together stitch the underarm seam, then press.

3 Turn right side out and run a gathering thread around the top of the sleeve.

4 Pull up the gathering thread until the sleeve fits neatly.

5 Turn under raw edge and slipstitch sleeve in place.

Shoes

1 Cover the back of the shoe leather with tacky glue and stick to the bottom of the doll's foot. Overlap one back piece over the other to create back seam.

2 Clip excess around foot and turn under and glue to bottom of foot.

3 Cut a rectangle of leather larger than sole of foot and glue to bottom of foot as a sole. Leave to dry.

4 When dry trim away excess leather around the sole.

5 Trim the top of the shoe with a buckle.

Wig

Wig your doll using platinum or white viscose. Dress hair in a small ponytail tied with a black ribbon. Add a couple of rolls of hair to each side of the head just above the ears.

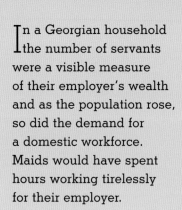

In a Georgian household the number of servants were a visible measure of their employer's wealth and as the population rose, so did the demand for a domestic workforce. Maids would have spent hours working tirelessly for their employer.

Materials

Female doll in her
    underwear
Cotton fabric for dress
Cream fabric for under
    sleeves
White cotton for apron
    and cap
Lace edging
Paint for shoes
Tacky glue
Viscose wigging

Georgian Housemaid

EVERY GEORGIAN DOLLS' HOUSE NEEDS A MAID TO KEEP IT LOOKING CLEAN AND PRISTINE. THIS HARD-WORKING SERVANT IS THE PERFECT CHOICE.

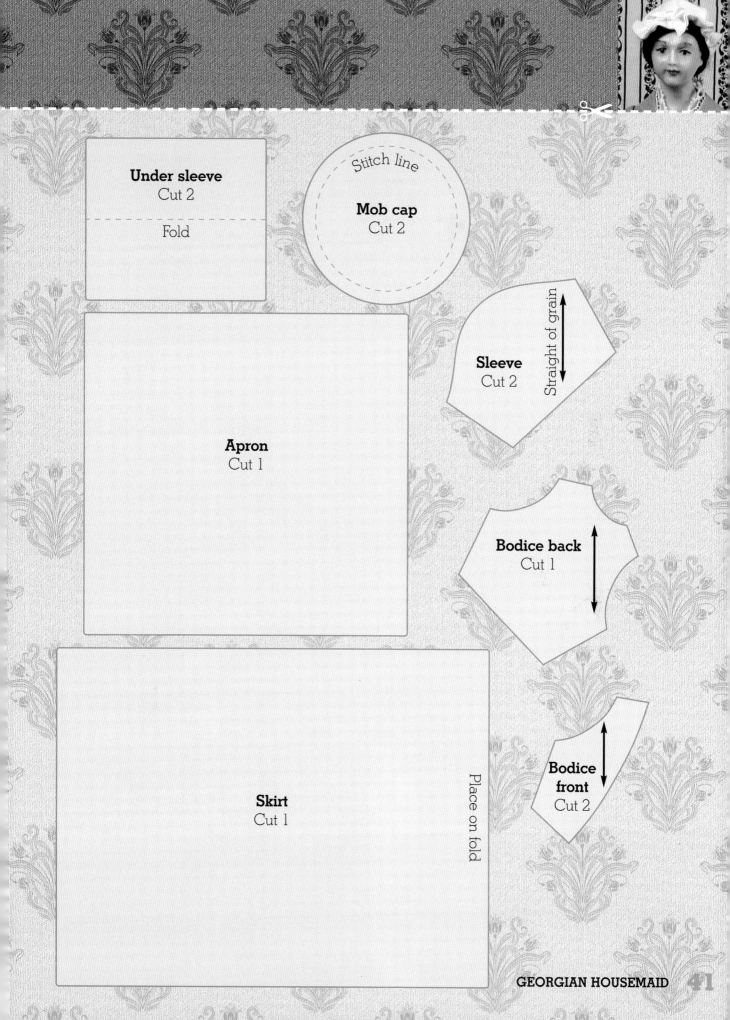

Under sleeve
Cut 2

Fold

Stitch line

Mob cap
Cut 2

Straight of grain

Sleeve
Cut 2

Apron
Cut 1

Bodice back
Cut 1

Skirt
Cut 1

Place on fold

Bodice front
Cut 2

Preparation

Trace pattern pieces and check the sizes against your doll. Make any adjustments that are needed. To make sure of the fit and construction make up pattern in kitchen paper first. When happy with the pattern pieces lay them out on the relevant fabric, remembering to reverse the pieces where necessary. Draw round patterns with either tailor's chalk or erasable fabric pen. Then run a thin beading of tacky glue along the pattern lines and allow to dry. This stops the fabric from fraying. Cut out pattern pieces.

Paint shoes in desired colours. If acrylics are used a coat of varnish will be needed to seal the paint.

Skirt

1 Turn up the hem and stitch.

2 Stitch the centre back seam – a French seam will give a neater finish.

3 Run a gathering thread around the waist, fit onto your doll. Pull up the gathers arranging them neatly around the doll's waist.

Under Sleeve

1 Fold the under sleeve in half along the fold line.

2 Stitch the short sides together to form a tube.

3 Run a gathering thread around the top (raw edge).

4 Slipstitch onto the dolls' arm about half way up.

5 Pull up the gathering thread and secure.

Bodice

1 With the right sides facing stitch the side and shoulder seams and press.

2 Turn in the raw edge along both fronts and around the neck. Trim with lace edging.

3 Fit the bodice onto the doll, crossing the right front over the left.

4 Turn under the raw edge at the waist and slipstitch the bodice to the skirt.

Sleeve

1 With the right sides together stitch the underarm seam and press. Turn the sleeve the right way out.

2 Run a gathering thread around the top of the sleeve.

3 Fit the sleeve onto the doll, pull up the gathering thread until a good fit is achieved.

4 Turn under the raw edges and stitch the sleeve in place.

5 Fold up the under sleeve over the raw edge of the top sleeve.

Apron

1 Turn in the raw edge on all four sides and glue or sew in place.

2 Run a gathering thread along the top edge. Pull up until it fits the doll's waist.

3 Stitch apron into place.

Mob Cap

1 Dress the hair in a simple style as most of it will be covered by the cap.

2 Make a small slit in the middle of one piece of the mob cap (this will be the inside of the cap).

3 With the right sides together stitch round the edge of the cap on the stitching line.

4 Turn the cap the right sides out through the slit that you made earlier. Press.

5 Run a small gathering thread around the cap. Pull up the gathers until a good fit is achieved.

6 Secure the cap to the head with a small amount of glue.

The Edwardian era saw a rising interest in the plight of the poor and in particular the social status of women. George Bernard Shaw's popular 1912 play *Pygmalion* explores these themes with the well-loved character of Eliza Dolittle.

Materials

Female doll in tatty
  underwear
Cotton fabric for coat
Cotton fabric for skirt
Cotton fabric for apron
  and blouse
Aged lace (see below)
Bead button
Charcoal (optional)

Flower Seller

THIS HUMBLE FLOWER SELLER'S COSTUME REFLECTS HER HARD WORKING LIFE. THE WORN AND AGED FABRICS CREATE THE PERFECT EFFECT.

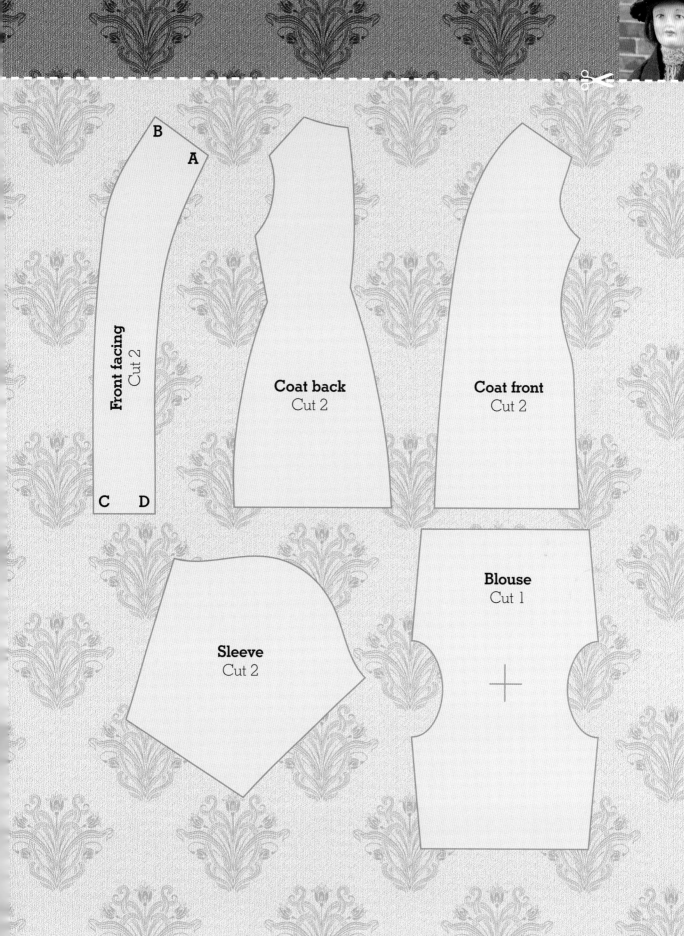

B
A

Front facing
Cut 2

C   D

Coat back
Cut 2

Coat front
Cut 2

Sleeve
Cut 2

Blouse
Cut 1

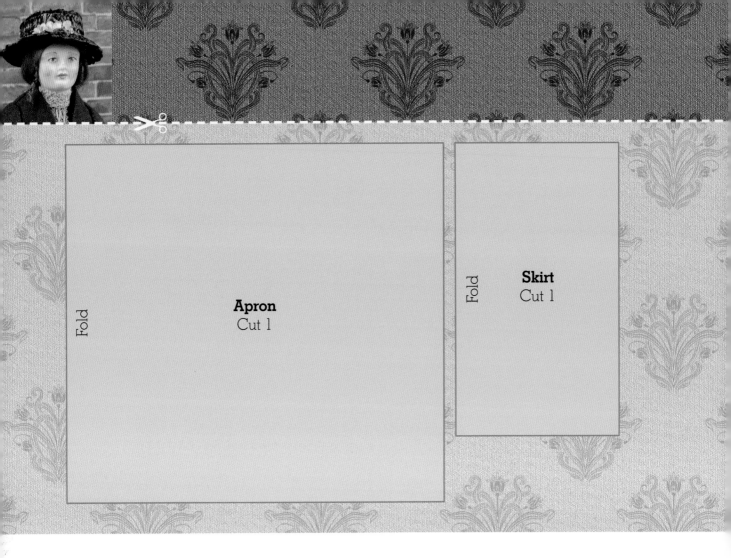

Fold

Apron
Cut 1

Fold

Skirt
Cut 1

Preparation

Trace pattern pieces and check for size against your doll. Make any necessary adjustments. To make sure of fit or construction make the pattern up in kitchen paper first. Once happy with your pattern pieces lay them out on the relevant fabric, remembering to reverse the pattern pieces where necessary. Draw round pattern with either tailor's chalk or erasable fabric pen. Run a thin beading of tacky glue along pattern lines and allow to dry before cutting out. (This helps to prevent fabric fraying.) Paint boots in desired colour using either enamel or acrylic paints, remembering that if acrylics are used a coat of varnish will be needed to seal the paint.

How to Age Lace

White cotton lace can easily be aged or made to look dirty by dipping it in a solution of black tea or coffee. Dampen the lace in water first, this helps it take up a more even colour. Dip into black tea/coffee and swish it around. Leave in for just a moment to get an ecru colour. You can always re-dip it if necessary. Leave in for longer to get a darker colour. The strength of tea or coffee will have some bearing on the eventual colour.

Once you have achieved your required colour (don't forget it will dry lighter), squeeze out the excess liquid and leave to dry. Once dry lightly iron to remove any creases.

Blouse

1 Cut neckline (as indicated on the pattern) large enough for doll's head to go through.

2 With right sides together stitch one side seam. Press.

3 Fit the blouse onto your doll.

4 Fold under seam allowance on front bodice and glue, or stitch side seam closed.

5 Trim the front of blouse with a strip of lace.

6 Glue another strip of lace around doll's neck. A frill of lace can also be glued around the dolls' wrists to indicate sleeve cuffs.

Skirt

1 Turn up hem and stitch or glue in place, and press.

2 Sew up back seam and press seam open.

3 Run a gathering thread around the skirt waist.

4 Fit skirt onto your doll, over the blouse. Pull up the gathering thread and secure.

5 Arrange the gathers neatly, pushing most of the fullness to the sides and back.

Apron

1 Hem the bottom of the apron.

2 Hem both sides of the apron.

3 Run a gathering thread along top of apron. Pull gathers up slightly so that the apron fits comfortably to the front of the skirt. Stitch or glue in place.

Coat

1 Stitch centre back seam and press.

2 With right sides facing, stitch front facing to front, from A–B–C–D.

3 Trim corners at B and C. Turn right side out and press.

4 Stitch side seams and press.

5 Stitch shoulder seams and press.

6 Turn up hem along bottom of coat and glue in place.

7 Turn under raw edge at back of neck and glue in place.

8 Fit coat onto your doll and stitch closed at front with a bead button.

Coat Sleeves

1 Measure sleeve against doll and hem cuff.

2 Stitch underarm seam and then press.

3 Turn sleeve right side out and run a gathering thread around top of sleeve.

4 Fit sleeve onto doll, pull up the gathering thread until a good fit is achieved.

5 Turn in raw edges and slipstitch sleeve in place.

Finishing Touches

Style the doll's hair in a simple bun with a centre parting. Give the doll a simple straw hat and a large basket to carry her flowers.

Pedlars, or tinkers, were travelling sellers of an assortment of household goods. Sometimes they worked door-to-door or at fairs and market places. This costume is inspired by the nursery rhyme, 'Tinker, Tailor, Soldier, Sailor...'

Materials

Older female doll in
   underwear
Cotton fabrics
Lace trimming
Assorted ribbons
Picot braid
Strip of leather
Basket
Assorted fabric scraps
Assorted sewing items

Tinker

TINKERS, PEDLARS AND HAWKERS SOLD THEIR WARES FROM DOOR-TO-DOOR, AND WERE ONCE A VERY COMMON SIGHT IN TOWNS AND VILLAGES ACROSS THE LAND.

Preparation

Trace pattern pieces and check for size. To make sure of fit make up in kitchen paper. Once happy with your pattern pieces lay them out on the relevant fabric. Draw round pattern with tailor's chalk or fabric pen. Run a thin beading of glue along pattern lines and allow to dry before cutting out. Paint shoes or boots using either enamel or acrylic paint.

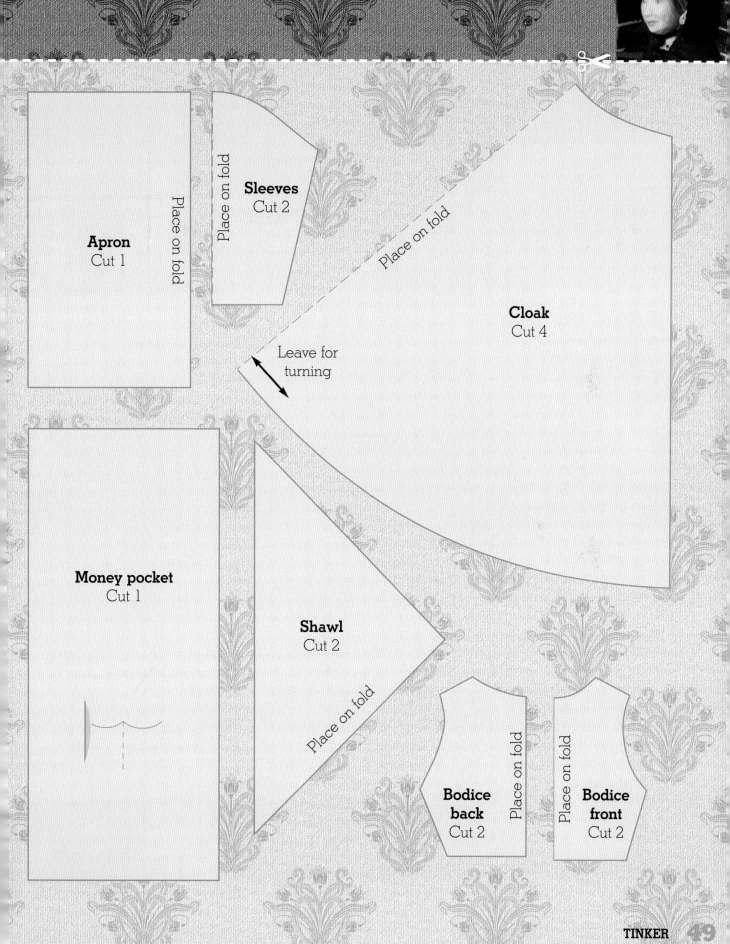

Apron
Cut 1

Place on fold

Sleeves
Cut 2

Place on fold

Place on fold

Cloak
Cut 4

Leave for turning

Money pocket
Cut 1

Shawl
Cut 2

Place on fold

Bodice back
Cut 2

Place on fold

Place on fold

Bodice front
Cut 2

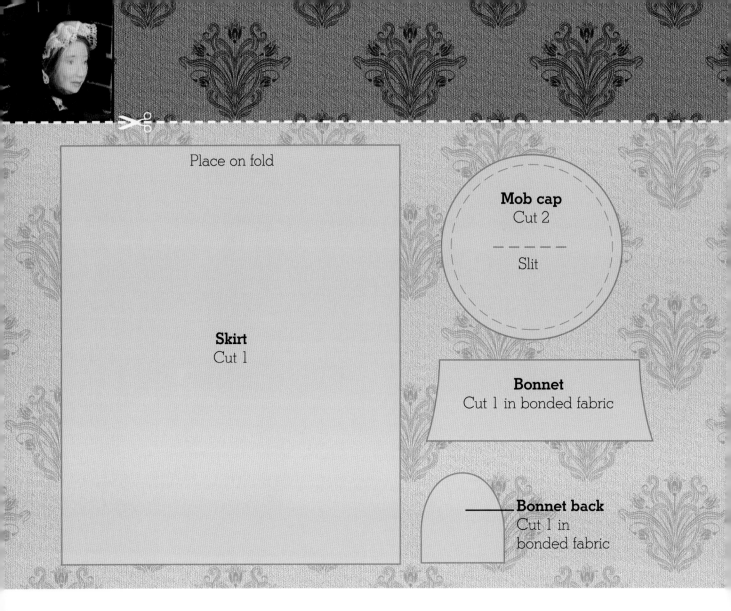

Skirt

1 Turn up hem and stitch.

2 Run a back seam (a French seam gives a neater finish) and press.

3 Run a gathering thread around the top of the waist. Fit onto doll, pull up gathers and secure. Then arrange the gathers neatly.

Bodice

1 Stitch side seams and shoulder seams and press.

2 Turn under raw edge on one of the back pieces, and raw edge around the neckline.

3 Fit bodice onto doll and slipstitch back closed.

4 Turn under raw edge around waist and slipstitch bodice to skirt.

Sleeves

1 Turn up excess length and stitch or glue in place.

2 With right sides facing, stitch underarm seam. Press.

3 Turn the sleeves the right side out, and run a gathering thread around the top.

4 Fit the sleeves onto the doll, pull up the gathering thread.

5 Turn under raw edge and slipstitch sleeve in place. Trim the cuff with lace.

Shawl

1 Turn under the raw edge on the long side of the shawl. Fray both of the other sides.

2 Wrap the shawl around the doll, crossing the ends over the chest. Secure in place.

Apron

1 Turn under and hem both short sides.

2 Turn under and hem the bottom and press.

3 Fold over the raw edge at the top and bottom.

4 Run a gathering thread along the top edge of the apron, and gather up to fit waist. Stitch or glue in place.

Money Pocket

1 Fold pocket in half, with the right sides together, stitch both side seams then turn right side out and press.

2 Turn the folded end up to create a pocket and slipstitch the sides closed. Turn under the raw edge at the top.

3 Stitch in place at the doll's waist, over the apron.

Cloak

1 With right sides facing pin the cloak together.

2 Stitch all the way around the cloak as indicated on the pattern, leaving a turning gap along the hem.

3 Trim seams close to stitching, clip curves and snip across the corners.

4 Fix ribbon ties to the top of the cloak and fit to your doll.

Mob Cap

1 Make a small slit in the middle of one piece of the cap (this will be the inside).

2 With right sides together, stitch around the edge of the cap.

3 Turn right sides out through the slit that you made earlier, and press.

4 Add lace trimming to the edge of the cap.

5 Run a small gathering thread around the cap, pull up the threads until a good fit is achieved. Secure to head with a small drop of glue.

Bonnet

1 Cut the two pattern pieces out of bonded fabric. If you don't have Bondaweb to hand glue some fabric to both sides of a thin piece of card and cut the pattern pieces from that.

2 Apply a thin beading of glue around the arch of the crown piece. Glue the back to the brim. Use a large marker pen or similar as a block to help support the pieces while the glue sets. Leave to dry.

3 Trim all edges around the crown with picot braid.

4 Glue ribbon ties to the inside of the hat and decorate as you wish.

5 Fit hat onto doll's head over the mob cap and tie ribbons under the doll's chin.

Basket

1 Cut the handle off the basket.

2 Fill basket with trimmings etc. gluing the items in place. Arrange bought items in prominent positions.

3 Cut a thin strap of leather and glue it to the sides of the basket. Fit around the doll's neck.

This brown warehouse coat could be used in several different shops from general stores and greengrocers, to hardware shops. The coats were also commonly used by other tradesmen such as removal men or delivery men.

Materials

Male doll
White cotton fabric (shirt)
Black fabric (trousers)
Cotton fabric (overalls)
Ribbon (tie)
Bondaweb
Beads (buttons)

Shopkeeper

THIS SHOPKEEPER IS A JAUNTY CHARACTER FOUND IN A VARIETY OF STORES INCLUDING GREENGROCERS, HARDWARE AND CORNER SHOPS.

Preparation

Trace the pattern pieces and check for size against your doll. Make any necessary adjustments. Make up the pattern in kitchen paper first to make sure of the fit or construction.

Once happy with your pattern pieces lay them out on the relevant fabric, remembering to reverse the pieces where necessary. Draw around the patterns with either tailor's chalk or erasable fabric pen. Run a thin beading of tacky glue along the pattern lines

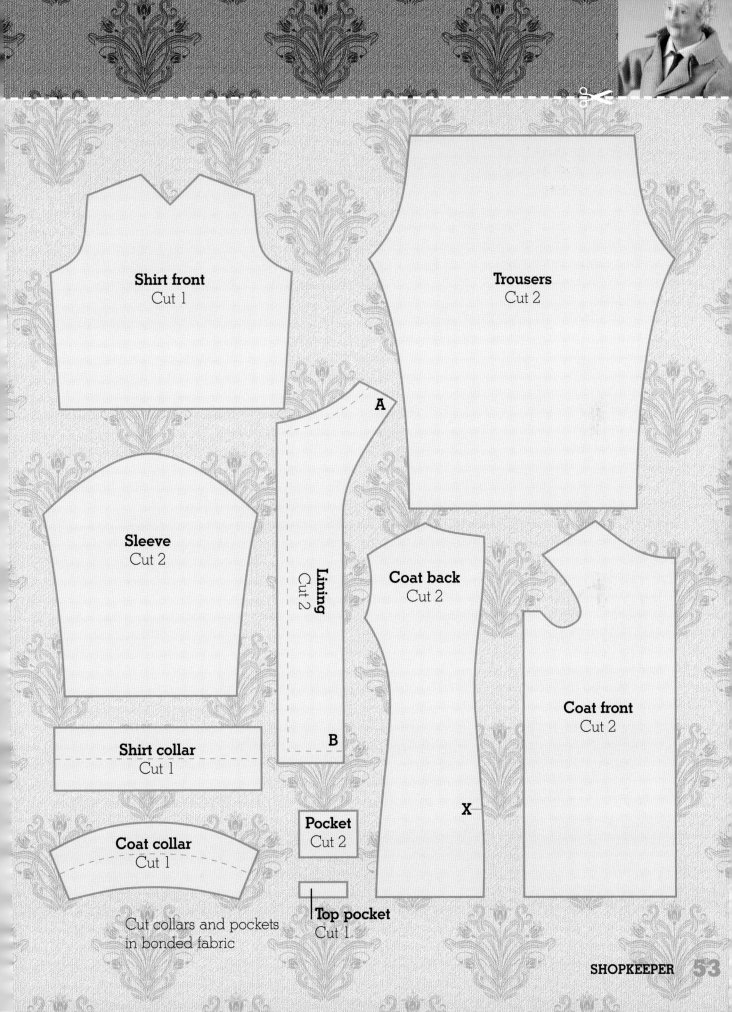

Shirt front
Cut 1

Trousers
Cut 2

Sleeve
Cut 2

A

Lining
Cut 2

B

Coat back
Cut 2

Coat front
Cut 2

X

Shirt collar
Cut 1

Pocket
Cut 2

Coat collar
Cut 1

Top pocket
Cut 1

Cut collars and pockets
in bonded fabric

and allow to dry. This helps to stop the fabric from fraying. Cut out the pattern pieces.

Paint the shoes or boots in desired colour with either acrylic or enamel paint (apply a coat of varnish if using acrylic paint to seal).

Shirt

1 Fold along the collar fold line as indicated. Clip to the fold line at several intervals along one side of the collar.

2 Place around the doll's neck and check the fit (adjust if necessary).

3 Apply glue to the clipped side of the collar; glue the unfolded collar around the doll's neck.

4 Glue or sew the shirt onto the doll, covering the clipped part of the collar.

5 Tie a ribbon tie around the doll's neck and fold down the collar.

Trousers

1 Stitch centre front and back seam, clip curve and press seam open.

2 Check the length of the trouser against your doll and turn up hems.

3 Stitch the inner leg seams.

4 Clip seam at crotch to stitching line, then turn trousers right side out and press.

5 Turn under raw edge at waist and run a gathering thread around the waist.

6 Fit onto the doll and pull up the gathering thread to fit the doll's waist and secure.

Overall Coat

1 Stitch the centre back seam to point 'X' as marked on the pattern. Press the seam open, including the back vent. Glue the vent seams in place.

2 With the right side facing, stitch jacket front and lining together from A–B.

3 Trim the seam fairly close to the stitching line, clip curves.

4 Turn the front right side out and press.

5 Stitch the side seams and then press.

6 Stitch the shoulder seams and press.

7 Turn up the bottom hem.

8 Fold and press the collar along the line marked on the pattern. Clip the collar to the fold line in several places.

9 Sew or glue the collar in place and fit the coat onto the doll.

10 Lap the left front over the right and stitch in place.

11 Stitch bead buttons down the coat front and glue the pockets in place.

Coat Sleeves

1 Measure the sleeve against the doll's arm and turn up the cuff.

2 With the right sides together stitch the underarm seam and press. Turn the sleeve the right way out.

3 Run a gathering thread around the top of the sleeve, and fit onto the doll. Pull up the thread until a good fit is achieved.

4 Make sure that the raw edges are turned under and slipstitch the sleeve in place.

Be inspired by your favourite group or singer. Why not create a recording studio with gold discs on display. Or, make miniature posters and CDs, a wardrobe of stage costumes, a selection of guitars, and other accessories that the rock star would have.

Materials

Male doll
Lightweight denim
** fabric**
White cotton
Black leather for
** waistcoat and belt**
Beads
Belt buckle

Rock Star

THIS FUN CHARACTER WEARS THE CLASSIC JEANS AND LEATHER WAISTCOAT COMBINATION TO MAKE HIM LOOK LIKE A REAL ROCK STAR.

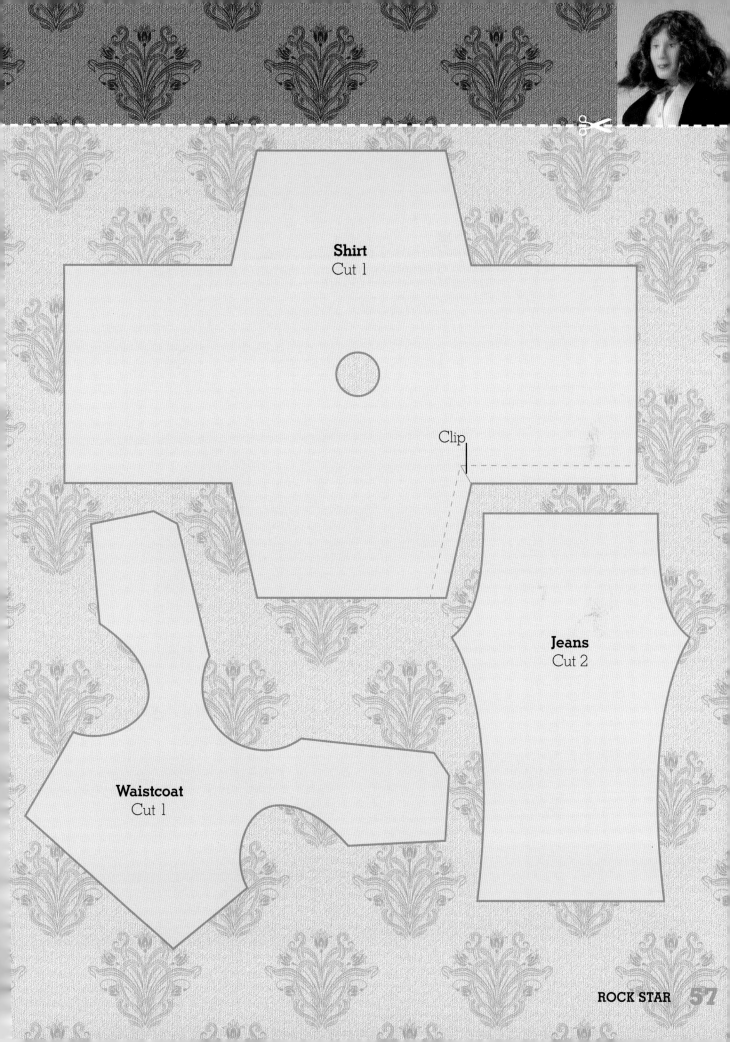

Shirt
Cut 1

Clip

Jeans
Cut 2

Waistcoat
Cut 1

Preparation

Trace pattern pieces and check for size against your doll. Make any necessary adjustments. To make sure of fit or construction make the pattern up in kitchen paper first. Once happy with your pattern pieces lay them out on the relevant fabric, remembering to reverse pattern pieces where necessary. Draw round pattern with either tailor's chalk or erasable fabric pen. Run a thin beading of tacky glue along pattern lines and allow to dry before cutting out to help prevent the fabric fraying. Paint shoes or boots in desired colour using either enamel or acrylic paints, remembering that if acrylics are used a coat of varnish will be needed to seal the paint.

Shirt

1 Turn up a hem at the end of each sleeve.

2 Fold under raw edge along both fronts.

3 Neaten raw edge around the neck.

4 Stitch the underarm and side seams.

5 Clip seam at underarm as shown on pattern and press seams flat.

6 Turn shirt right sides out and fit shirt onto doll

7 Glue or slipstitch the front of the shirt closed. Add bead buttons and roll up the sleeves.

Jeans

If you want the jeans to be tight-fitting, make seams wider than the recommended amount.

1 With right sides together stitch front and back crotch seam, clip curve and press the seam open.

2 Stitch inner leg seams. Clip seam and turn jeans right side out and press.

3 Fit onto doll and run a gathering thread around waist; pull up to fit and secure.

4 Make a belt from a strip of leather, add a buckle and glue in place around doll's waist.

Waistcoat

Cut waistcoat from leather. Glue or stitch side seams and fit onto doll.

Finishing Touches

Wig your doll in your preferred style. Add a multi-coloured bead necklace.

In the Country

Traditional morris dances have been around in England since the 15th century and were originally performed by men, but nowadays they can be performed by everybody. This morris dancer is in the more familiar white outfit, but their outfits can be as varied as the dance groups themselves. There are groups who perform in white shirts and black trousers, some wear long white socks, while others wear brightly coloured waistcoats, and their sashes and ribbons come in all colours, as do the various styles of hat.

Materials

Male doll
White cotton for trousers
White cotton lawn for shirt
White beads for buttons
Strip of leather for belt
Scrap of leather for bell belt
Gold seed beads
Bondaweb
Black fabric
Ribbon for sashes
Flowers and feathers for hat decoration

Morris Dancer

THIS JAUNTY MORRIS DANCER IS THE PICTURE OF RUSTIC TRADITION AND COUNTRY LIVING. HE WEARS ONE OF MANY VARIATIONS OF THIS COSTUME.

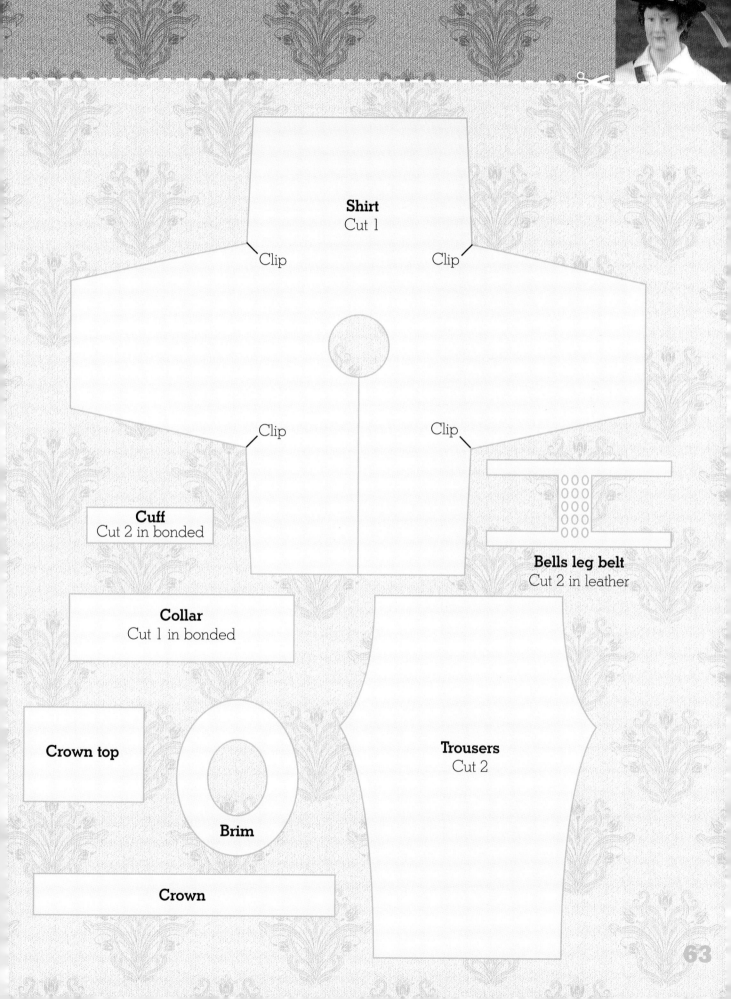

Shirt
Cut 1

Clip   Clip

Clip   Clip

Cuff
Cut 2 in bonded

Bells leg belt
Cut 2 in leather

Collar
Cut 1 in bonded

Crown top

Brim

Trousers
Cut 2

Crown

Preparation

Trace pattern pieces, and check for size against your doll. Make any necessary adjustments. To make sure of fit or construction make the pattern up in kitchen paper first. Once happy with your pattern pieces lay them out on the relevant fabric, remembering to reverse the pattern pieces where necessary. Draw around patterns with either tailor's chalk or erasable fabric pen. Then run a thin beading of tacky glue along the pattern lines and allow to dry. This helps to stop the fabric from fraying. Cut out pattern pieces. Paint shoes or boots in desired colour using either enamel or acrylic paints. If acrylic paints are used a coat of varnish will be needed to seal the paint. Bonded fabric in this pattern refers to two pieces of fabric bonded together with an iron on fusing product such as Bondaweb.

Shirt

1 Turn under a small hem along both front edges.

2 Fold shirt with right sides together and then stitch the underarm and side seams in one. Repeat for the other sleeve.

3 Clip seam at underarm as shown on pattern and press seams flat. Turn shirt right sides out.

4 Cut collar out of bonded fabric. Fold it in half lengthwise and press.

5 Clip at intervals along one side of collar to fold line.

6 Place collar around doll's neck to check the fit. Adjust fit if necessary.

7 Apply glue to the clipped portion of the collar and glue unfolded collar around doll's neck. Leave to dry.

8 Fit the shirt onto doll, lapping the left-hand side over right and slipstitch front closed. Add bead buttons and fold down collar.

9 Run a gathering thread around each sleeve at the cuff. Pull up gathering thread and secure.

10 Cut cuffs out of bonded fabric and then glue cuffs in place.

Trousers

1 Stitch centre front and back seam, clip curve and press.

2 Check trouser length against doll and turn up hems.

3 Stitch inner leg seams and clip seam at crotch. Turn trousers right side out and then press.

4 Run a gathering thread around waist and fit the trousers onto doll. Pull up the thread to fit the waist and secure.

5 Make a belt from a strip of leather and glue in place around waist, adding a buckle for decoration.

Bell Belts

Cut belts from leather and sew on seed beads as shown on pattern. Fit the belts to doll's leg, glue in place.

Hat

1 Cut hat pieces from bonded fabric.

2 Bend crown into an oval shape a little larger than the hole in the centre of the brim. Glue ends in place (trim if necessary). Leave to dry.

3 Glue crown in place on brim and leave to dry.

4 Glue crown top on top of the crown and leave to dry.

5 Once dry trim crown top flush with crown sides.

Finishing Touches

1 Wig doll's hair in desired style.

2 Add ribbon sashes to doll.

3 Decorate hat with ribbons, flowers and feathers.

4 Cut sticks from cocktail sticks or give him white handkerchiefs to wave.

In 1884 Maud Watson became the first Ladies Wimbledon Champion. The daughter of a rector, she was one of thirteen competitors and beat her sister Lillian in the final 6–8, 6–3, 6–3. This pattern is an interpretation of what she wore taken from an old photograph. This pattern could equally be used as an everyday outfit for a lady, just make the skirt a little longer.

Materials

Female doll in her
    underwear
White cotton fabric for
    the blouse
Patterned fabric for skirt
White lace for
    decoration
Paint for shoes
Straw hat

Tennis Player

WHAT BETTER WAY TO SPEND A COUNTRY BREAK THAN PLAYING A GAME OF TENNIS? THE CRISP WHITE BLOUSE AND FULL SKIRT LOOK VERY FETCHING.

Blouse front
Cut 2

Skirt
Cut 1

Place on fold

Gather

Apron
Cut 1

Gather

Sleeve
Cut 2

Blouse back
Cut 1

Preparation

Trace pattern pieces, and check for size against your doll. Make any necessary adjustments. To make sure of fit or construction make the pattern up in kitchen paper first. Once happy with your pattern pieces lay them out on the relevant fabric, remembering to reverse the pattern pieces where necessary. Draw around patterns with either tailor's chalk or erasable fabric pen. Then run a thin beading of tacky glue along the pattern lines and allow to dry. This helps to stop the fabric from fraying. Cut out pattern pieces. Paint shoes in desired colour using either enamel or acrylic paints. If acrylic paints are used a coat of varnish will be needed to seal the paint.

Blouse

1 With right sides together, stitch side seams.

2 Press seams open and stitch shoulder seams, then press them again.

3 Slip the blouse onto the doll and make any adjustments that are necessary.

4 Overlap right front over left and slipstitch closed.

5 Add lace trimming to front of blouse and around the neck.

6 Measure sleeve for length against the doll and turn up a small hem at the cuff.

7 With right sides together stitch the underarm seam and press, then turn sleeve right side out.

8 Run a gathering thread around top of sleeve.

9 Fit sleeve onto doll; pull up gathering thread until a good fit is achieved.

10 Turn in raw edge and slipstitch sleeve to bodice.

Skirt

1 Measure skirt against doll for length. Turn up hem.

2 With right sides of fabric facing, stitch centre back seam and press seam open.

3 Run a gathering thread around waist of skirt.

4 Fit skirt onto doll; pull up gathering thread to fit and then secure.

5 Arrange gathers evenly around doll's waist.

Apron

1 Turn up hem and stitch centre back seam. Press seam open.

2 Run gathering threads down both sides of apron as marked on pattern.

3 Run a gathering thread around waist of apron.

4 Fit apron onto doll over skirt and gather up waist until a good fit is achieved. Arrange most of the fullness to the back of the skirt.

5 Pull up gathering threads at the side of the apron and then secure.

6 Arrange folds around the apron as desired. Stab stitch or glue in place if desired.

Waistband

Cover the raw edge at the waist with a waistband made either with a strip of ribbon or a strip of the same fabric as the skirt, with all the raw edges turned under. Glue or stitch waistband in place.

Finishing Touches

Wig your doll in your chosen hairstyle. Finish outfit with a straw boater.

Many agricultural labourers wore smocks in the 18th and 19th centuries, as they were so practical. Smocks were made of up to 8yds (7m) of heavy white linen, therefore the garment stood away from the body which meant that it shed rain easily (they were also windproof). Labourers took great pride in their smocks often wearing them outside of working hours. Smocks were usually embroidered with elaborate designs, the style was different from county to county.

Materials

Male doll
White/off white fabric
Fabric for trousers
Scrap of fabric for
  necktie
Cream seed beads
Leather/paint for boots
Bondaweb

Shepherd

THIS LOYAL SHEPHERD WEARS HIS SMOCK WITH PRIDE.
HE MAKES A STRIKING IMAGE OF THE JOYS AND
HARDSHIPS OF COUNTRY LIFE.

Sleeve
Cut 2

Collar
Cut 1 in bonded fabric
Fold

Stitching lines

Smock back
Cut 1

Seam line

Seam line

Trousers
Cut 2

Stitching lines

Smock front
Cut 2

Fold line

Seam line

Fold

Yoke
Cut 1

Preparation

Trace pattern pieces and check for size against your doll. Make any necessary adjustments. To make sure of fit or construction make the pattern up in kitchen paper first. Once happy with your pattern pieces lay them out on the relevant fabric, remembering to reverse pattern pieces where necessary. Draw round pattern with either tailor's chalk or erasable fabric pen. Run a thin beading of tacky glue along pattern lines and allow to dry (to help prevent fabric fraying) before cutting the pieces out.

Paint boots or shoes in desired colour using either enamel or acrylic paint, add a coat of varnish to seal if using acrylic paint. Here the man's boots were covered in thin leather to give the texture of a workman's boots.

Trousers

1 With right sides facing, stitch front and back crotch seam. Clip curve and press the seams open.

2 Turn up a hem on both legs, then stitch the inner seam.

3 Clip the inner seam then turn the trousers right side out and press.

4 Fit the trousers onto your doll. Run a gathering thread around the waist; pull up to fit and secure.

Necktie

Make a necktie from a scrap of fabric and tie it around your doll's neck.

Collar

1 Cut a collar from bonded fabric (two pieces bonded together with a fusible product such as Bondaweb).

2 Fold the collar along the fold line indicated on the pattern and press.

3 Clip to the fold line in several places along one side of the collar.

4 Try the collar around the doll's neck, adjust the length or fit as necessary.

5 Apply glue to the clipped part of the collar.

6 Fit the collar around the doll's neck over the necktie, allow to dry.

Once the yoke has been fitted the collar will be folded down.

Smock

1 Using a basic decorative stitch on your sewing machine stitch four rows of decorative stitching on the back and front rows of the smock.

2 With right sides together stitch the side seams up to the point marked on the pattern. Press the seams open.

3 Stitch the front seam to just below the decorative stitching. Press the seam and slightly overlap the left front over the right.

4 Turn up a hem and press.

5 Run separate gathering threads along each row of fancy stitching.

6 Try the smock on your doll and pull up the gathering threads until a good fit is achieved around the chest. Secure all gathering threads.

Yoke

1 Fold under a tiny amount of raw edge down both fronts.

2 Fold under the raw edge along the bottom of the yoke, on both front and back. Slipstitch the yoke in place.

3 If the yoke is gaping over the shoulders take a small tuck across the shoulder and glue down (like a mock shoulder seam).

4 Fold down the collar, and stitch bead buttons down the front of the smock.

Get into the country theme with this Provençal dress. It could be used as the basic pattern for any countrified woman of lower status from the mid-18th century to Victorian times.

Materials

Female doll in her
    underwear
Light-coloured cotton
    fabric for blouse
Patterned cotton fabric
    for skirt
Fabric for shawl
Coloured fabric for
    apron
9/32in (7mm) wide ribbon
    for apron
    and waistband
Fine cotton fabric for cap
Small amount of lace

Rural Woman

THIS RURAL WOMAN WILL FIT INTO ANY COUNTRY SCENE PERFECTLY, WITH HER RUSTIC BASKET, SHAWL AND PRETTY CAP.

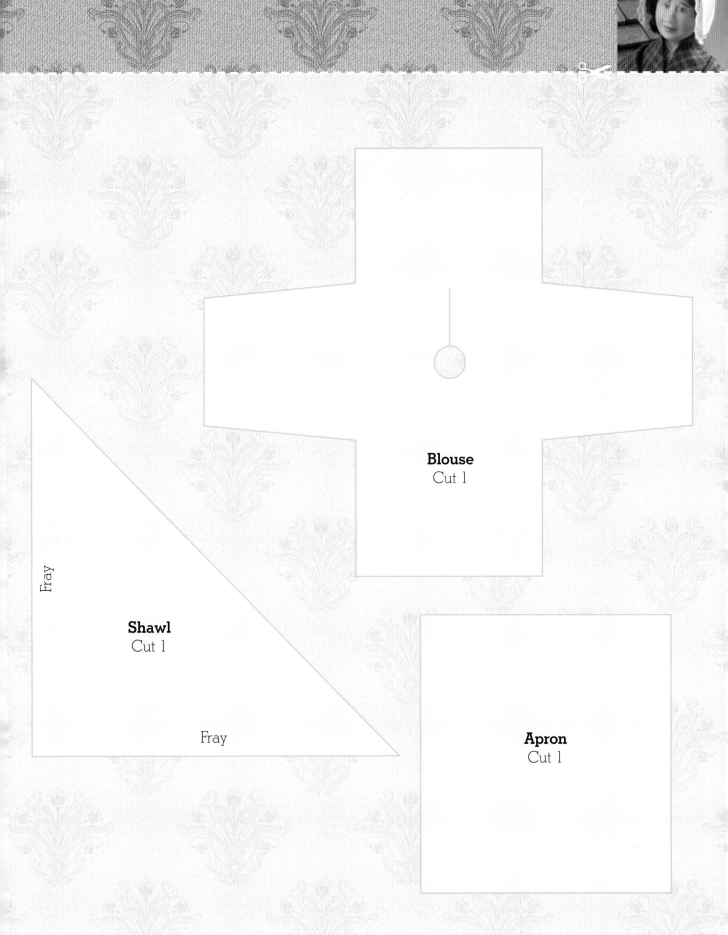

Blouse
Cut 1

Shawl
Cut 1

Fray

Fray

Apron
Cut 1

Preparation

Trace pattern pieces and check for size against your doll. Make any necessary adjustments. To make sure of fit or construction make the pattern up in kitchen paper first. Once happy with your pattern pieces lay them out on the relevant fabric, remembering to reverse pattern pieces where necessary. Draw round pattern with either tailor's chalk or erasable fabric pen. Run a thin beading of tacky glue along the pattern lines and allow to dry before cutting out. (This helps to prevent fabric fraying.)

Paint shoes or boots in desired colour using either enamel or acrylic paints, remembering that if acrylics are used a coat of varnish will be needed to seal the paint.

Blouse

1 With right sides facing, stitch underarm and side seam in one.

2 Clip seam at underarm and press seams open. Turn right side out and press again.

3 Fit blouse onto doll and add a lace collar.

Skirt

1 Turn up hem and stitch.

2 Stitch back seam (a French seam gives a neater finish) and press.

3 Run a gathering thread around top of waist and fit the skirt onto doll, pull up gathers and secure, arranging the gathers evenly around the waist.

Shawl

1 Turn under raw edge on long side of shawl.

2 Fray both of the other sides.

3 Wrap shawl around doll's shoulders, crossing the ends over the chest and secure in place.

Wigging

Wig the doll in any style you would like.

Apron

1 Turn under and hem both short sides.

2 Turn under and hem the bottom and press.

3 Run a gathering thread along top edge of apron and gather up to fit waist of doll.

4 Stitch or glue in place.

5 Add a ribbon waistband and tie around doll's waist leaving ties to hang down the back.

Cap

1 Place the two pieces of the cap brim together with right sides facing.

2 Stitch around brim leaving a gap open between the two crosses as marked on the pattern.

3 Clip around the edge to facilitate turning.

4 Turn brim the right side out and press.

5 Run a gathering thread around the crown.

6 Pull up thread so that the crown fits the back of the doll's head.

7 Sew or glue brim to the crown. (A small gap at the back of the crown will be left. Turn the raw edge under at that point.)

8 Fit cap onto doll and lightly glue in place.

Special Occasions

This dress was inspired by looking through the bridal magazines in a local newsagent's for ideas to dress a contemporary bride. There were many influences of Gothic, Medieval and Georgian styles of dress, but nothing that seemed to be of 'now'. The traditional stiff skirt in ivory silk is teamed with a wine-red bodice and carries the contemporary feel with a short perky veil and a dark red and cream bouquet.

Materials

Female doll with full
    porcelain arms and
    legs
Silk dupion in bodice
    colour
Silk dupion in
    ivory/cream
Cotton lawn
Lace edging
Bondaweb
Enamel or acrylic paint
    for shoes
Viscose hair
Fine nylon netting
Silk ribbon for roses
Gold metal thread and
    pendant (optional)

Wedding Dress

THIS BRIDE LOOKS STUNNING IN HER SOPHISTICATED GOWN WHICH COMBINES OLD-FASHIONED SENTIMENT WITH A CONTEMPORARY TWIST.

Preparation

Trace pattern pieces and check the sizes against your doll. Make any necessary adjustments. To make sure of the fit and construction make up pattern in kitchen paper first. When happy with the pattern pieces, lay them out on the relevant fabric, remembering to reverse the pieces where necessary.

Bodice
Cut 1
in silk

Straight grain

Place on fold

Skirt
Cut 1

Neat
end

**Bodice
liner**
Cut 1 in
cotton

Place on fold

Petticoat
Cut 1

Draw round patterns with either tailor's chalk or erasable fabric pen. Then run a thin beading of tacky glue along the pattern lines and allow to dry. This stops the fabric from fraying. Cut out pattern pieces. Paint shoes in desired colours. If acrylics are used a coat of varnish will be needed to seal the paint.

Petticoat

1 Turn up the hem. Attach lace to bottom of petticoat.

2 Stitch centre back seam and then press.

3 Run a gathering thread around the waist of the petticoat.

4 Fit onto doll, pulling up the gathers and arranging around the waist.

5 Spray petticoat with a fine mist of hairspray and allow to dry. This will give a good stiff petticoat to hold out the bridal skirt.

Dress

1 Turn under hem and secure.

2 Stitch centre back seam and then press.

3 Run a gathering thread around the waist of the skirt and fit onto doll.

4 Pull up the gathering thread and then secure. Arrange gathers evenly around the doll's waist.

Bodice

1 Bondaweb the bodice liner centrally onto the bodice, leaving an allowance all round.

2 Clip bodice allowance from the raw edge to the liner, particularly around the curved edges.

3 Turn under all the raw edges and glue in place.

4 Fit the bodice onto the doll, starting at the centre front and wrapping tightly around the doll's torso. Stitch or glue into place.

5 Trim the bodice with bunka etc. as desired.

Veil

1 Wig the doll as you wish.

2 Make a veil from a piece of netting 5½in (14cm) by 3½in (9cm).

3 Fold in half and then run a gathering thread along the fold. Gather up tightly and secure.

4 Glue veil to the top of the doll's head and decorate (here with silk ribbon roses).

Finishing Touches

The bride has been given a heart pendant necklace and bouquet of red and cream roses. The necklace is a strand of gold machinery embroidery thread and the pendant came from a fair. The bouquet is made from paper flowers.

This lovely lavender tweed-effect fabric conjured up the idea of a mother in a stylish suit with pearl necklace. Perfect for a special wedding day.

Materials

Female doll in her
    underwear
Tweed-effect fabric
    for jacket and skirt
Beads (to match jacket
    fabric)
White pearl beads
    for necklace
Acrylic/enamel paint
    for shoes

Mother of the Bride

A PROUD MOTHER ON HER DAUGHTER'S WEDDING DAY NEEDS TO LOOK THE PART. THIS LOVELY LAVENDER TWEED SUIT WILL NOT LET HER DOWN ON THE BIG DAY.

Skirt
Cut 1

**Jacket
back**
Cut 2

A   B

**Jacket
facing**
Cut 2

C   D

Jacket front
Cut 2

Dart

Collar
Cut 1
on cross

Sleeve
Cut 2
on cross

Preparation

Trace pattern pieces, and check for size against your doll. Make any necessary adjustments. To make sure of the fit and construction make the pattern up in kitchen paper first. Once happy with your pattern pieces lay them out on the relevant fabric, remembering to reverse pattern pieces where necessary. Draw round patterns with either tailor's chalk or erasable fabric pen. Then run a thin beading of tacky glue along the pattern lines and allow to dry. This stops the fabric from fraying. Cut out pattern pieces. Paint shoes in desired colour using either enamel or acrylic paints, remembering that if acrylics are used a coat of varnish will be needed to seal the paint.

Skirt

1 Turn up the hem, stitch and then press.

2 With the right sides facing, stitch the centre back seam from the hem to mark. Press the seam open.

3 Slip the skirt onto the doll and slipstitch the remainder of the seam closed.

4 Run a gathering thread around the top of the skirt, pull up the excess of material around the waist and secure.

Jacket

1 Stitch the centre back seam and press.

2 Stitch the darts on both fronts and press towards the side seam.

3 With the right sides facing, place front facing onto jacket front. Stitch the jacket front and front facing from A–B–C–D.

4 Trim corners at B and C, and trim front seam. Turn right side out and press.

5 Stitch the side seam and then press.

6 Stitch the shoulder seam and press.

7 Turn lapels back and press into place. Turn up the bottom hem.

Jacket Collar

1 Fold the collar in half with the right sides together. Stitch both short ends.

2 Trim seams, turn right sides out and press.

3 Fold collar in half and then press lightly.

4 Using the fold crease as a guide, line up with the back of the jacket (underside of collar to wrong side of the jacket) and stitch in place.

5 Fold down the collar and then press.

6 Fit the jacket onto doll. Slipstitch jacket closed.

7 Sew or glue buttons in place

Sleeves

1 Measure sleeve against doll and turn up raw edge of cuff.

2 With right sides together underarm seam and press.

3 Turn sleeve right sides out. Run a gathering thread around the top of the sleeve.

4 Fit the sleeve onto the doll, pull up gathering thread until a good fit is achieved.

5 Turn in the raw edges and stitch in place.

Necklace

1 String white pearl beads onto white cotton thread until the desired length is achieved.

2 Tie off cotton in a triple knot close to the beads.

3 Add a dot of Superglue to the back of the doll's neck to hold the necklace in place.

The idea for this gold evening dress came from a Sunday magazine supplement. It is an easy pattern with only two pieces. The top of the dress is contrived by wrapping a piece of fabric around the doll and tucking in the raw end. Together with the skirt it creates a contemporary style, but you could add a net skirt for a 1950s feel.

Materials

Female doll with full
  porcelain legs and
  arms
Silk dupion in chosen
  colour
Fringing to match dress
Enamel or acrylic paint
  for shoes
Gold metal thread and
  crystals for jewellery
Viscose hair
Very fine glitter
  (optional)
Fray check
Tacky glue

Birthday Outfit

A SPECIAL OCCASION REQUIRES A SPECIAL OUTFIT AND
THIS STUNNING DRESS WILL NOT FAIL TO IMPRESS FOR
A ROMANTIC BIRTHDAY DINNER.

Bandeau top
Cut 1

Skirt
Cut 1

Preparation

Trace the pattern pieces and check the sizes against your doll. Make any necessary adjustments. To make sure of the fit and construction make up your pattern in kitchen paper first. When happy with the pattern pieces lay them out on the relevant fabric, reversing the pieces where necessary. Draw round patterns with either tailor's chalk or erasable fabric pen. Then run a thin beading of tacky glue along the pattern lines and allow to dry. This stops the fabric from fraying. Cut out pattern pieces. Paint shoes in desired colours. If acrylics are used, a coat of varnish will be needed to seal the paint.

The Dress

1 As the top and bottom of the dress will not be seen, treat with fray check.

2 With right sides together, stitch the centre back seam, and press.

3 Fit onto doll, partway up bust line and glue in place.

4 Add fringing to hemline.

Bandeau Top

1 With right sides together, fold in half lengthways.

2 Using the seam allowance, stitch lengthways along the raw edge. Then press the seam flat.

3 Turn the right sides out and press again with the seam along the centre back.

4 Start at the middle of the back, wrap around the front, under the armpit and over the breasts, under the other armpit and around to the back again.

5 Then wrap around again, dropping lower under the first breast, around the front and up and over the opposite shoulder, tucking the raw end down between the layers at the back, after trimming to length first. Stitch or glue in place.

6 Stitch or glue top to dress where needed.

7 A little bead of glue over the top of the arm may be needed to hold the shoulder piece in place.

Hair

1 The doll is wigged in a fashionable contemporary style, starting with a basic ponytail, but twisting the tail up the back of the head (gluing in place) and when dry cutting the tail so it is short and spiky.

2 Use a short burst of hairspray to set the spiky top and while still moist sprinkle on very fine glitter.

Accessories

1 Make a necklace from fine gold metallic embroidery thread, glued in place.

2 Make a bracelet by using the same thread around the wrist a few times and gluing in place. Several crystals were used as decoration.

The lace chosen for this project is beautiful and freely available. When making the bonnet, it proved to be just perfect as it formed a lovely little crown quite by chance. Any similar ¼in (6mm) lace with a scalloped edge would be suitable.

Materials

Pongee silk fabric for skirt lining and sleeves
7in (177mm) square of silk tulle
Narrow lace trim
⁵⁄₆₄in (2mm) silk ribbon
2 tiny embroidery beads for buttons
Cutting mat and rotary cutter
Cutting grid
Needle and thread
Fray check and 00 or 0 paintbrush

Christening Gown

DAINTY AND INTRICATE, THIS LACY GOWN WILL MAKE A PERFECT CHRISTENING DAY OUTFIT FOR A BONNY, BEAUTIFUL BABY.

Sleeves
Cut 2 in pongee

**Bodice
right back**
Cut 1 in
pongee

Fold
line

**Bodice
left back**
Cut 1 in
pongee

Fold
line

Bodice front
Cut 1 in pongee

Place on fold

Lining
Cut 1 in pongee

Back seam

Length as required

Place on fold

Overskirt
Cut 1 in silk tulle

Back seam

Length as required

Gown

Note: the skirt and lining are formed as two seperate pieces for steps 1 to 4 inclusive. This helps to cut down on the bulk when gathering the skirt to add to the bodice, which can often distort the 1:12 scale proportion of the item.

1 Cut out the skirt lining, sleeves and bodice back and front from pongee and the tulle overskirt. Paint the edges with the tiniest amount of fray check and leave to dry.

2 Using a small running stitch, sew the gathering rows in the front and back of both pieces.

3 Sew a $\frac{1}{8}$in (3mm) back seam in the lining and overskirt finishing off about $\frac{1}{2}$in (12mm) from the top edge of the skirts as shown on the pattern pieces. Open out and gently press with the fingertips.

4 Starting at the back seam of each, sew the narrow lace trim into place around the lower hem, turning under $\frac{1}{4}$in (6mm) to finish off.

5 Pull up the gathering threads on the front parts of the lining and overskirt until they fit the lower edge of the bodice. Secure the threads and lay the overkirt over the lining. Tack them carefully together then with right sides together, sew the double layered skirt to the lower part of the bodice. Gently press the bodice upwards.

6 Starting at the lower edge of the bodice, cover it with lace, stitching each row of lace in turn across the upper edge of the lace only, leaving the scalloped edge of the lace free. See diagram 1 on facing page.

7 Attach the bodice backs in the same way, leaving $\frac{1}{8}$in (3mm) for turning under on the right side of the bodice back and $\frac{1}{4}$in (6mm) on the left side, this is $\frac{1}{8}$in (3mm) for turning under and $\frac{1}{8}$in (3mm) for the overlap when sewing on the buttons. See diagram 2. Cover with lace strips as for the bodice front, and join the shoulder seams.

8 Carefully trim the lace around the neckline and oversew the edge with a tiny blanket stitch.

9 Sew the gathering rows on the two sleeves and trim the lower edge with narrow lace.

10 Sew the two sides of the sleeves together with a $\frac{1}{8}$in (3mm) seam.

11 Pull the gathering threads gently and starting at the top of the sleeve and working down the front bodice to the underarm, attach it to the bodice with a tiny ladder stitch. Stitch the remaining part of the sleeve to the bodice back. Repeat for the other sleeve.

12 Overlap the left back over the right and secure into place by attaching the two tiny beads for buttons. Make a tiny bow from some silk ribbon with two fairly long tails and attach it to the front of the gown.

Bonnet

1 To make the bonnet, cut five strips of narrow lace 2in (50mm) long. Using diagram **3** as a guide and starting with the straight back, lay the strips under each layer whilst stitching them in place as you go. At the two sides of the bonnet, allow the strips to curve in slightly for the neckline keeping the back of the bonnet straight and allowing a gentle curve at the front.

2 Fold the bonnet in half and close the back seam just slipstitching the two straight edges of the lace together on the wrong side, in order to create a flat back.

3 Turn through to the right side and you will see that the scalloped edge of the lace you have just sewn at the back of the bonnet will stand out to form the crown.

4 Sew a tiny blanket stitch around the neckline to finish it off which will also neaten the cut ends of the lace. Add two long ribbons for ties.

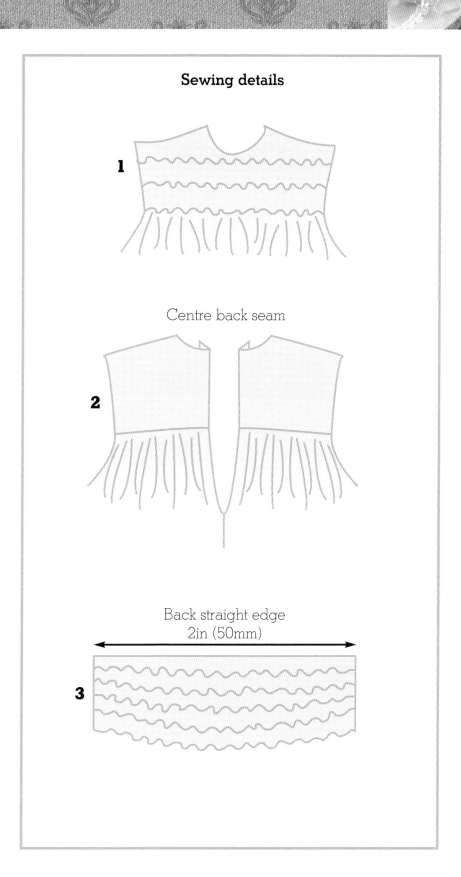

Sewing details

1

Centre back seam

2

Back straight edge
2in (50mm)

3

Fancy Dress

Anna Pavlova was one of the greatest classical ballerinas of the early 20th century. This pattern is based on a dress style that featured in over fifty short ballet pieces, which Anna created and performed to display a particular ballet technique known as 'divertissements'. The costume is in contrast to the more traditional tutus and classical floating creations we are usually accustomed to.

Materials

3ft x 6in (1m x 152mm) approx of silk tulle
Small quantity of ivory lace cotton trim
1 x Dylon cold water dye in sea-green and fixer
Sea-green organza
Lightweight iron-on interfacing
Double-sided interfacing for the wings
Aquamarine designer glitter dust
Glitter adhesive
Small piece of tan leather for slippers
$\frac{5}{64}$in (2mm) aqua silk ribbon
Sea-green thread
Thick designer PVA glue
Fray check and a fine paintbrush

Ballerina

INSPIRED BY THE RUSSIAN BALLERINA ANNA PAVLOVA, THIS BEAUTIFUL BALLET COSTUME MAKES FOR SOME MAGICAL DRESSING UP.

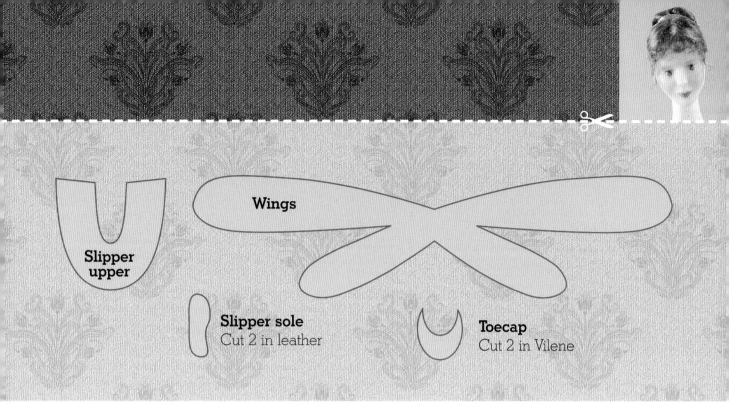

Slipper upper

Wings

Slipper sole
Cut 2 in leather

Toecap
Cut 2 in Vilene

Dyeing Silk Tulle

If dyeing your own silk tulle, follow the instructions included with the dye carefully. Whilst making up a dye bath you may find it useful to include some other fabric or lace to use at a later date for a project of your own. When dyeing silk tulle and lace, it is best to dye from ivory for the best results as white is often bleached and this can affect the outcome and overall success of the dyeing process. Always remember to allow for a little shrinkage when dyeing. Dye both the silk tulle and the narrow ivory lace for your dragonfly.

The Dress

1 Cut one strip of tulle 32in x 2in (81cm x 50mm) for the underskirt of the dress and one strip 32in x 2in (81cm x 50mm) for the overskirt. Lay the strips in turn on some kitchen roll and paint all edges with fray check. Always remove the tulle after painting the edge as it will stick to the kitchen roll if you leave it to dry there and wash out the brush immediately in warm soapy water.

2 Sew a neat gathering row of running stitches ⅛in (3mm) down from the upper edge of each strip. Pull the gathers gently on each strip and leave to one side. Do not tie off your threads at this stage. There is no need to sew a back seam in the tulle skirt layers as there is sufficient width to conceal the back opening and the icicles will cover this area.

3 Cut a piece of organza approx. 8in x 3in (203mm x 76mm) and iron a piece of lightweight interfacing onto it. Cut out 16 long dress 'icicles' from this fabric and 14 tiny arm band icicles. Apply a little fray check to all the edges.

4 Apply a fine line of glitter adhesive to one of the long sides of each icicle then sprinkle with the aquamarine glitter dust. Leave all the icicles to dry thoroughly. It is easier to put the slippers on now before attaching the dress.

Slippers

1 Glue one edge of some aqua ⁵⁄₆₄in (2mm) silk ribbon at right angles to the arch of the doll's foot. Bring the ribbon across the top of the foot, round the back and once around the ankle. Then across the top of the foot in the opposite direction and glue the end back under the arch of the foot.

2 Cut out the slipper uppers in aqua silk and apply fray check to all edges.

3 Cut out the Vilene toecap and position it ⅛in (3mm) down from the neckline of the slipper and iron it on. Clip the inner front curves of the neckline to the Vilene taking care not to cut past the fray check, fold down the clipped curves and glue them evenly to the Vilene. Turn down and press ⅛in (3mm) hem around the entire slipper neckline.

4 Join the back of the slipper with a ⅛in (3mm) seam and the hem open. Press the seam open, turn down the hem and glue it into place on the back seam.

5 Run a tiny gathering stitch around the lower edge of the slipper where the sole is to be attached. Fit the slipper onto the foot and gently pull the gathering thread. Work the silk with your fingertips and stitch the slipper into place with some zigzag stitches across the length of the foot. Fasten off the thread.

6 Cut out two soles in leather. Apply a little glue to the stitching on the slipper and the sole. Gently ease into position. If required, dab a little glue to the actual foot to hold the slippers on.

Dress

1 Using the dyed narrow lace, form a bodice underlay adding a strip at a time, starting around the upper bust and finishing with a strip just above the waistline. Secure each strip at the back with a little glue. I used the same lace and method to make pantaloons to cover the cloth thigh of the doll.

2 Fit the shorter tulle underskirt around the doll about ¼in (6mm) in down from the waist and fasten off the thread. Use a dressmaker's pencil or tailor's chalk to make a small mark where the top of the skirt is to sit. Apply a thin line of glue around this mark and attach the skirt so that it is edge to edge at the back.

3 Repeat for the longer tulle overskirt attaching it in higher than the first, so that it sits neatly on the waist.

4 Attach each icicle in turn with designer PVA around the upper waistline, overlapping them as you go.

5 Cut a rectangle of dyed silk tulle, 3in x 2in (76mm x 50mm). Turn under one long edge and glue the centre of it to the centre of the bust over the lace. Leave to dry.

Armbands

Glue the tiny icicles around the upper arm edge to edge. Glue a small piece of the ribbon around the top edge of the icicles.

6 Gather the remaining tulle with your fingertips, turning the bottom hem under and secure with a little glue at the doll's sides. Gently pull the tulle before gluing to ensure a neatly gathered bodice.

7 At the back of the bodice, gently pull the left side and secure into place at the centre back and trim any surplus tulle. Turn the other side under, trimming any surplus and secure over the left side.

8 Glue one edge of some $5/64$in (2mm) aqua silk ribbon just above the bust on the left-hand side and cross and secure it to the underside of the bust on the right-hand side. Repeat in reverse so they form a cross in the centre. Glue another piece of the ribbon, starting and finishing at the back around both the upper and lower edges of the tulle bodice, over the ends of the crossed ribbon. You can place an optional silk ribbon rose at the centre of the cross, with two ribbon tails, if you wish.

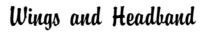

Wings and Headband

1 Sandwich together two pieces of organza large enough for the wing pattern, with some double-sided interfacing and cut out the wings when cool. Gently fold in half to find the centre then open out again

2 Apply a very fine line of glitter adhesive to the upper edge of the, wings with the fold line pointing upwards and dust with the aquamarine glitter dust. Attach the centre line of the wings to the centre back of the doll with the fold line pointing into her back.

3 Finally, attach a small piece of aqua ribbon around the front of the hair top knot and either leave it plain or add a silk rose or some glitter dust to it.

101

The characterization of a thief in striped top and dark eye patches has cropped up in countless comic books, computer games and nursery rhymes. From dear old 'Burglar Bill' to the children's fortune-telling rhyme 'Tinker, Tailor...' this enduring image remains.

Materials

Plump male doll
Black cotton
Striped cotton jersey
9/32in (7mm) wide black ribbon
Bondaweb
Fabric for sack

Thief

WHETHER THIS CHARACTER REMINDS YOU OF COMIC BOOKS OR NURSERY RHYMES, IT HAS A FUN AND LIGHT-HEARTED FANCY DRESS LOOK.

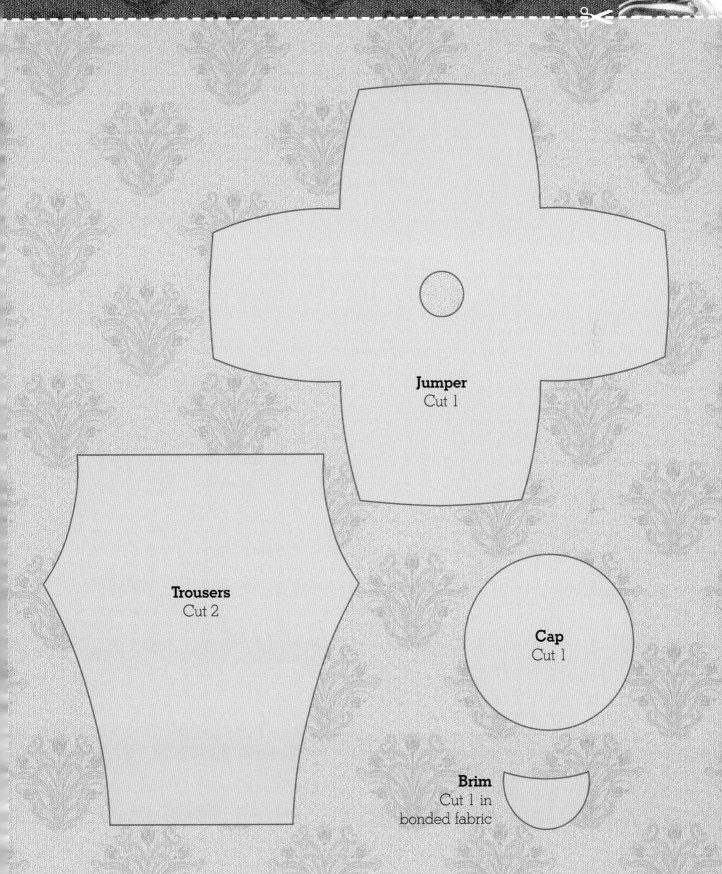

Jumper
Cut 1

Trousers
Cut 2

Cap
Cut 1

Brim
Cut 1 in
bonded fabric

Preparation

Trace around the pattern piece and check the size against your doll. Make any necessary adjustments. Make up the pattern in kitchen paper first to make sure of the fit or construction. Once happy with the pattern pieces lay them on the relevant fabric, remembering to reverse them where necessary. Draw round the pattern with either tailor's chalk or erasable pen. Run a thin line of tacky glue along the pattern lines and allow to dry before cutting out (to prevent the fabric from fraying). Paint shoes or boots in desired colour using either enamel or acrylic paint. Seal acrylic with a coat of varnish.

Trousers

1 With the right sides together seam the front and back crotch seam, clip curve and press seam open.

2 Turn up the hem on both of the legs.

3 Stitch the inner leg seam. Clip, and turn the trousers the right side out and press.

4 Fit the trousers onto the doll. Run a gathering thread around the waist, pull up to fit and secure.

Jumper

1 Turn up hem on the front and back of jumper.

2 Fold under a raw edge at the end of each sleeve.

3 Fold under raw edge around the neck.

4 Fold the jumper with the right sides together, stitch sleeve and side seam in one. Repeat for the other side and then press.

5 Fit the jumper onto the doll, easing the head through the neck hole. Try not to stretch the fabric too much.

Mask

1 Bond together two short pieces of the $^{9}/_{32}$in (7mm) wide ribbon. Round off the two ends.

2 Cut out eyeholes and a triangular cut for the nose.

3 Glue on ribbon ties and fit onto doll.

Cap

1 Run a gathering thread around the edge of the cap.

2 Pull up the gathers and check the fit against your doll, adjusting gathers as required to reduce or enlarge the size.

3 Glue the peak of the cap in place.

4 Glue the whole hat to the doll's head.

Swag Bag

1 Cut a piece of fabric 3½in x 2¾in (9cm x 7cm).

2 Turn under one long raw edge and fold the fabric in half, wrong sides together.

3 Stitch the bottom and side seams and turn the right side out.

4 Write the word 'swag' onto the bag with a black felt tip.

5 Add a teaspoon of rice to the bag to give it weight.

6 Gather the top of the bag closed, adding a necklace or other 'booty' poking out the top for authenticity if you wish.

Finishing Touch

Add some suitable facial hair to your doll after wigging in whatever hairstyle you prefer.

In 1880, *The Pirates of Penzance* (or *The Slave of Duty*) by Gilbert and Sullivan was first shown in London. George Grossmith Jnr played the comic character Major General Stanley. The production includes many memorable musical numbers and is still popular today.

Materials

Male doll
Black cotton
Red cotton
Assorted gold braids
Gold beads
$5/64$in (2mm) gold ribbon
White and black paint
Black felt
Feathers
Sword

Major General

THIS PATTERN IS BASED ON GILBERT AND SULLIVAN'S COMIC OPERA, *THE PIRATES OF PENZANCE*. IT IS SET IN VICTORIAN TIMES AND SO THIS MILITARY GENT COULD EASILY GRACE ANY VICTORIAN HOUSEHOLD.

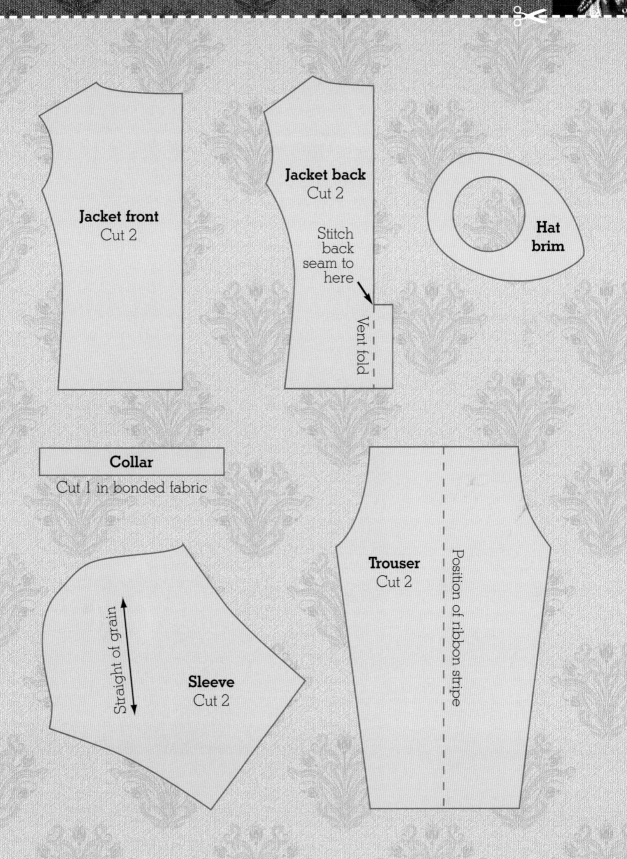

Jacket front
Cut 2

Jacket back
Cut 2

Stitch back seam to here

Vent fold

Hat brim

Collar
Cut 1 in bonded fabric

Straight of grain

Sleeve
Cut 2

Trouser
Cut 2

Position of ribbon stripe

Preparation

Trace pattern pieces and check for size against your doll. Make any necessary adjustments. To make sure of fit or construction make the pattern up in kitchen paper first.

Once happy with your pattern pieces lay them out on the relevant fabric, remembering to reverse pattern pieces where necessary. Draw round pattern with either tailor's chalk or erasable fabric pen. Run a thin beading of tacky glue along pattern lines and allow to dry before cutting out, this helps to prevent fabric from fraying.

Paint the boots black and gloves white using either enamel or acrylic paint. If acrylic paint is used then a coat of varnish will also be required.

Trousers

1 Using the silk ribbon, glue a gold stripe down the side of each trouser leg.

2 Stitch centre front and back seam. Clip curve and press seam open.

3 Turn up hem on each leg. Stitch inner leg seam, clip seam, turn and press.

4 Fit trousers onto the doll and glue in place around waist.

Jacket

1 With right sides together, stitch centre back seam to point marked on pattern. Press seam open.

2 Fold in vent flap on one side of jacket back, clip seam to stitch line and lay the other vent flap flat. Press vent.

3 Stitch side seams and press.

4 Stitch shoulder seams and then press.

5 Turn back raw edge on left front opening. Trim with gold braid.

6 Sew on gold bead buttons.

7 Turn under a very small amount on right front.

8 Fit jacket onto doll, glue or sew front opening closed, lapping the left front over the right.

Collar

1 Cut collar from two pieces of fabric bonded together.

2 Glue braid onto collar.

3 Glue collar around doll's neck covering raw edge of jacket neckline.

Sleeve

1 Check the sleeve for length against your doll's arm and turn up cuff.

2 Stitch seam and press.

3 Decorate cuff of sleeve with some braid.

4 Run a gathering thread around top of sleeve, fit sleeve onto doll and pull up gathering thread until sleeve fits neatly. Turn under raw edge and glue or slipstitch sleeve to jacket.

Hat

The hat was made from black felt, the crown was a piece of dampened felt stretched over a bottle top and secured with an elastic band, this was allowed to dry and then stiffened with fabric stiffener, allowed to dry again and then removed from the former.
I trimmed the crown to the desired height and glued it onto the brim. The side of the brim were then turned up and the whole hat stiffened again. I used curled feathers and a jewellery finding to decorate.

Finishing Touches

1 Cross $5/32$in (4mm) wide silk ribbon and gold braid across doll's chest, finishing each one crossed at alternate hips. Use another braid around the waist to hang the sword from.

2 Use another gold braid to make shoulder decorations, turn the raw edges under and glue in place.

3 The row of medals were made from a piece of ribbon, gold embroidery thread and four small circles punched from a piece of leather and coloured gold with a gold gel pen.

4 The doll is wigged with viscose with extra curly bits added as sideburns sweeping down into a handlebar moustache.

This little girl is dressed as the Queen of Hearts from *Alice in Wonderland* for a fancy dress party, but you can always leave aside the crown and sandwich board to leave the lovely party frock. I have used a craft punch and velvet to make the pattern on the skirt, but you can always substitute a patterned fabric instead.

Materials

Child doll
White dupion silk
Dark red silk
White cotton organdy/
    stiff fabric
Silk netting (optional)
Leather (optional)
Velvet paper
Small heart-shaped craft
    punch

Queen of Hearts

THE QUEEN OF HEARTS COSTUME IS A DELIGHTFUL FANCY DRESS OUTFIT FOR YOUR LITTLE GIRL, WHO WILL ALSO LOVE THE PRETTY DRESS UNDERNEATH.

Petticoat
Cut 1

Skirt
Cut 1

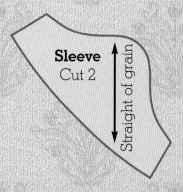

Sleeve
Cut 2

Straight of grain

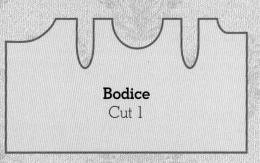

Bodice
Cut 1

Preparation

Trace pattern pieces and check for size against your doll. Make any necessary adjustments. To make sure of fit or construction make the pattern up in kitchen paper first.

Once happy with your pattern pieces lay them out on the relevant fabric, remembering to reverse pattern pieces where necessary. Draw round pattern with either tailors chalk or erasable fabric pen. Run a thin beading of tacky glue along pattern lines and allow to dry before cutting out. (This helps to prevent fabric fraying.)

Petticoat

1 Cut the petticoat from the white cotton organdy and turn up the hem, trimming it with lace.

2 Stitch the back seam and then press.

3 Run a gathering thread around the waist and slip the petticoat onto the doll.

4 Pull up the gathering thread and secure, arranging the gathers around the waist.

Bodice

1 Stitch the shoulder seams and press.

2 Decorate the neckline with bunka or other trimming to cover the raw edge.

3 Fit the bodice onto the doll.

4 Turn under the raw edge on one side of the bodice back as marked on the pattern.

5 Turn under the raw edge around the waist.

6 Slipstitch or glue the back closed then slipstitch the bodice to the skirt.

Skirt

1 Turn up the hem and stitch the back seam and press.

2 Run a gathering thread around the waist, fit skirt onto doll.

3 Pull up the gathering thread tight around waist and secure.

Sleeves

1 Trim the raw edge of bottom of sleeve with lace.

2 Stitch the underarm seam and press.

3 Run a gathering thread around the top of the sleeve, fit onto doll and pull up the thread.

4 Slipstitch the sleeve to the bodice, tucking in the raw edge as you go.

5 Run a gathering thread around the bottom of the sleeve. Pull up the thread and secure to create a puffed sleeve.

Finishing Touches

1 Wig your doll in desired style.

2 Tie a sash around the doll's waist.

3 Punch small heart shapes from velvet paper and glue randomly onto the skirt.

4 Cover the doll's legs in silk netting to resemble lacey tights. You could paint on socks or stockings if you prefer.

5 Make leather shoes or paint shoes on instead using either enamel or acrylic paints, remembering that if acrylics are used a coat of varnish will be needed to seal the paint.

Crown

The crown was simply made from a strip of card glued into a circle and paint with gold paint. Decorate using the same velvet hearts as on the skirt.

Sandwich Board

1 Scan a playing card into a computer and reduce to 60%, and print onto card and cut out. You will need two copies. You may be able to find small or mini packs or playing cards that can be used. Use the Queen and the Jack of Hearts to provide the front and back images.

2 Lay both cards face down, head to head with a small gap between them.

3 Glue on ribbon straps from the two top corners attaching once card to the other.

4 Glue another length of ribbon across the centre of the front card, allowing enough loose at each side to act as ties.

5 Repeat for the back card.

6 Fit sandwich board onto doll and tie the straps.

A universal character, this fortune teller is perfect for appearing at a village fete, a booth on the pier or in a darkened parlour of a Victorian dolls' house. It may be fun to experiment with the various settings she can be found in and those who would be drawn to her.

Materials

Female doll in her
    underwear
White cotton lawn for
    blouse
Contrasting cotton
    fabrics for skirt
    and underskirt
Fabric for bodice
Trimming for skirt
Bunka trimming for
    bodice and blouse
Patterned silk for sash
    and headscarf
Jewellery finding for
    earring

Fortune Teller

CROSS THE PALM OF OUR FORTUNE TELLER WITH SILVER AND SHE WILL GAZE INTO HER CRYSTAL BALL AND FORETELL YOUR FUTURE. SHE MAY ALSO READ YOUR TEA LEAVES OR DABBLE IN A LITTLE PALMISTRY.

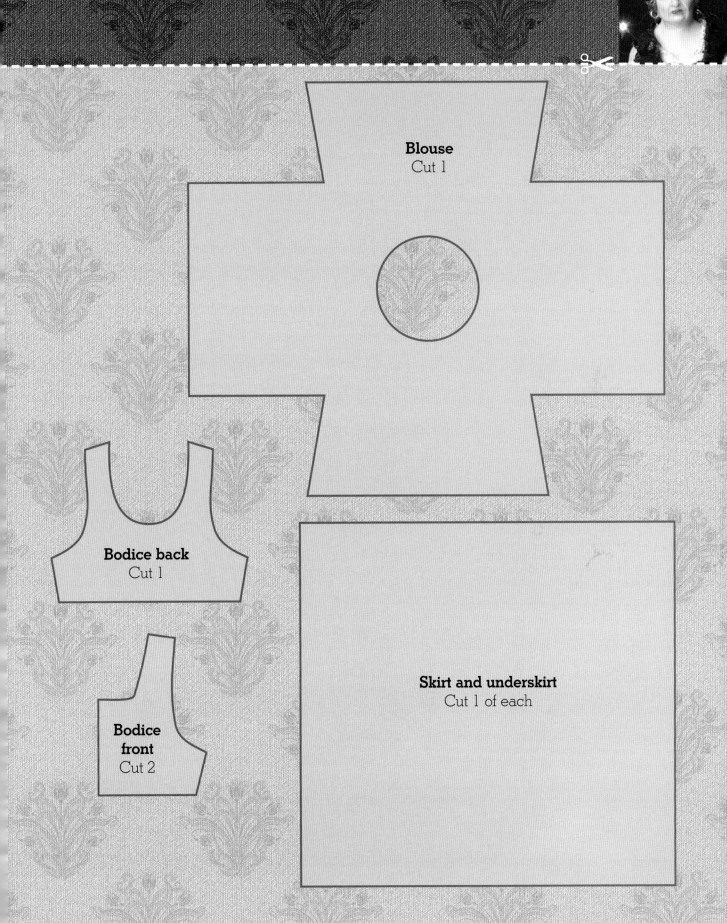

Blouse
Cut 1

Bodice back
Cut 1

Skirt and underskirt
Cut 1 of each

Bodice front
Cut 2

Preparation

Trace pattern pieces and check for size against your doll. Make any necessary adjustments. To make sure of fit or construction make the pattern up in kitchen paper first.

Once happy with your pattern pieces lay them out on the relevant fabric, remembering to reverse pattern pieces where necessary. Draw round pattern with either tailor's chalk or erasable fabric pen. Run a thin beading of tacky glue along pattern lines and allow to dry before cutting out to help prevent the fabric fraying.

Paint shoes or boots in desired colour using either enamel or acrylic paints, remembering that if acrylics are used a coat of varnish will be needed to seal the paint.

Blouse

1 Turn up a small hem at the end of each sleeve.

2 Trim around the neckline with Bunka.

3 With right sides facing stitch the underarm and side seam in one. Press seams.

4 Slip the blouse onto your doll. Run a gathering thread around the bottom of each sleeve, pull up and secure.

Underskirt

1 Turn up a hem.

2 Stitch the back seam and then press.

3 Check the skirt length against your doll, and adjust if necessary.

4 Run a gathering thread around the waist; slip the skirt onto your doll. Pull up the gathering thread and secure. Arrange the gathers evenly around the waist.

Skirt

This is worn shorter than the underskirt so check the length of skirt before you start and adjust the length if required.

1 Turn up a hem, and decorate the hemline. Fine zigzag braiding is used here.

2 Stitch the back seam and then press.

3 Run a gathering thread around the waist. Fit the skirt onto the doll, pull up the gathering thread and then secure.

Bodice

1 Stitch the side seams, the shoulder seams and then press.

2 Decorate the neckline and around the armholes with Bunka or other trimming.

3 Fit the bodice onto the doll and lace the bodice fronts together.

Sash

1 Take a length of silk fabric about 1½in (38mm) wide.

2 Fold the raw edge along both long sides and add a small piece of fringing to each end.

3 Tie the sash around the doll's waist and secure with a few small stitches.

Head

1 For the earring tie a small gold ring to a length of cotton. Glue this behind the doll's ear and take the cotton up and over the doll's head and down to the other ear. Attach another gold ring here. Glue the end of the thread to the top of the doll's head.

2 Wig the doll in any style, as all will be covered with a headscarf.

Headscarf

1 Cut from a small triangle of silk as for the sash.

2 Turn under all of the raw edges.

3 Trial fit the scarf onto the doll, lightly marking where the forehead comes on the scarf.

4 Attach gold coins or beads to the marked part of the scarf. The gold coins on the headscarf were made by punching out shapes, using an adjustable leather punch, from gold foil.

5 Fit the scarf, securing at the back of the head.

First found in the medieval Middle Eastern epic *1001 Arabian Nights*, the story of *Aladdin* is a worldwide children's classic that has crept into countless films, cartoons and TV programmes. The Genie character is bound to his magic lamp and is only released when lamp is polished and one of three wishes is made. Often, the moral of the story is to be careful what you wish for.

Materials

Male doll with full arms & half porcelain legs
White habotai silk
Patterned silk
Contrast silk for lining
Ribbon/silk for sash
1/16in (1.5mm) silk ribbon for turban
Gold embroidery thread
Leather
Gold paint
Feathers/jewels etc. for decoration

Genie

CREATE A MAGICAL AND MYSTICAL GENIE FOR AN ARABIAN NIGHTS ROOM BOX, OR TO ADD A TOUCH OF GLAMOUR TO A FANCY DRESS PARTY.

Preparation

The doll used for this project was poured in darker skin-toned porcelain, than the one usually used. Doll kits in this darker skin tone can be supplied but to order only.

Trace pattern pieces and check for size against your doll. Make any necessary adjustments. To make sure of fit or construction make the pattern up in kitchen paper first.

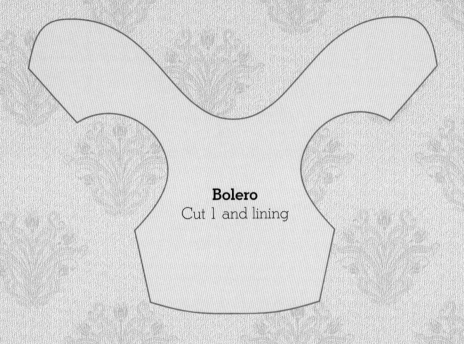

Bolero
Cut 1 and lining

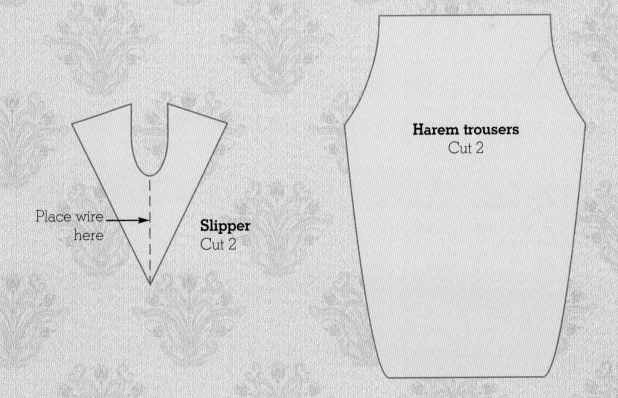

Harem trousers
Cut 2

Place wire here →

Slipper
Cut 2

Once happy with your pattern pieces lay them out on the relevant fabric, remembering to reverse pattern pieces where necessary. Draw round pattern with either tailor's chalk or erasable fabric pen. Run a thin beading of tacky glue along pattern lines and allow to dry before cutting out. This helps to prevent fabric fraying.

Bracelets

These are easier to do on the doll's arm before you put the doll together.

1 Dab a little superglue on the inside of the doll's arm.

2 Wind metallic gold thread around the arm to the width you require for your armlet. Start and end your winding on the inside of the arm.

3 Once the glue is dry paint glue or varnish over the thread for extra security.

Harem Trousers

1 Stitch centre front and back seam, clip curve and press seam open.

2 Turn up hem on each leg. Stitch inner leg seam, clip seam, turn and press. Fit trousers onto doll.

3 Gather bottom of each trouser leg. Glue in place around leg.

4 Cut a length of silk approx. 8½in x 1¼in (22cm x 3.5cm) for the sash.

5 Turn in the raw edge along both long sides of the sash. Fray the short ends.

6 Pleat the sash down the middle and fit sash around the waist.

Bolero

1 Cut one in your main fabric and one in your lining fabric.

2 With right sides together stitch all the way round the waistcoat leaving the bottom open.

3 Trim the seams and clip around the curves.

4 Turn right sides out, which can be a little tricky as the shoulders are quite narrow, use a blunt ended instrument to help you. Press.

5 Turn in raw edge along bottom and slipstitch closed. Slipstitch the side seams together.

Turban

1 Cut a length of silk. Turn in the raw edge on both long sides. Alternatively, use a piece of $1/16$in (1.5mm) wide silk ribbon, which stops the worry of raw edges.

2 Wrap around the doll's head several times, starting at the centre point of the silk at the back of the doll's head. Crossing over both ends at the front.

3 Tuck both ends in and glue in place.

Slippers

1 Cut the shoes from pale leather.

2 Glue a short piece of thin wire (I used paper-covered florist's wire) to the wrong side of the leather as indicated on the pattern. Allow to dry.

3 Cover the wrong side of the leather in tacky glue.

4 Place the leather on top of the doll's foot (make sure the front opening is positioned evenly on top of the foot).

5 Pinch the leather together behind the heel. Trim the leather flush to the back of the heel.

6 Pinch together along the sole of the foot.

7 Flattern the leather from the tip of the foot up to the point, making sure that you have an even margin of leather on each side reaching up to the point.

8 Trim the excess leather on the sole flush to the foot. Allow to dry.

9 With a pair of tweezers, roll up the tip of the shoe.

10 Paint the shoe in gold paint and allow to dry.

11 Varnish the shoe for added protection.

Finishing Touches

Decorate the front of the turban using jewellery findings, a feather and a gem.

This pattern is a version of the dress Marilyn Monroe wears in the infamous air vent scene of the film *Seven-Year Itch*. Of course, you don't have to pose your doll 'à la Marilyn', but the pattern is a typical 1950s-style halter neck dress and so could be used in a 1950s setting. It is also a very simple dress to make.

Materials

Female doll with full
    porcelain arms and
    legs
³⁄₈in (1cm) wide cotton
    lace
White habotai silk
¹⁄₁₆in (1.5mm) wide silk
    or soft ribbon
Thin wire

Marilyn Monroe

CREATE A STYLISH BUT SIMPLE 1950s HALTER-NECK
DRESS AND MAKE HEADS TURN WITH THIS MARILYN
MONROE-STYLE OUTFIT.

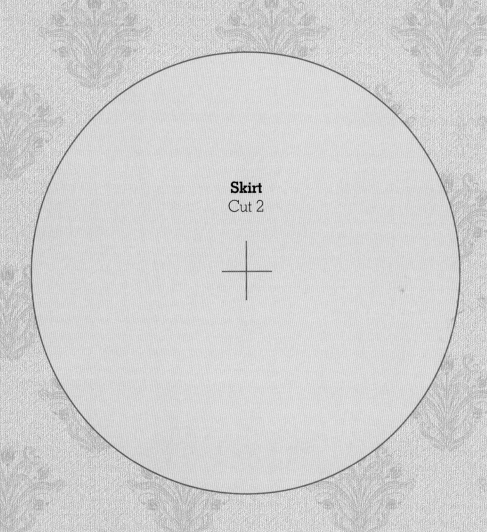

Skirt
Cut 2

Preparation

Trace pattern piece, and check for size against your doll. Make any necessary adjustments. To make sure of fit or construction make the pattern up in kitchen paper first.

Once happy with your pattern piece lay it out on the relevant fabric, remembering to reverse the pattern piece where necessary. Draw around with either tailor's chalk or erasable fabric pen. Then run a thin beading of tacky glue along the pattern lines and allow to dry. This helps to stop the fabric from fraying. Cut out pattern piece.

Paint shoes in desired colour using either enamel or acrylic paints. If acrylic paints are used a coat of varnish will be needed to seal the paint.

Underwear

1 Glue a strip of lace from just under the doll's belly button, down under her crotch and finish just below the small of her back. (It may be necessary to cut down the width of your lace for this part.)

2 Glue a second piece of lace from the front left side of the crotch, over the left leg and hip and down over half her bottom. (It will help if you cut a slight angle on either end of the lace.)

3 Then repeat for the right-hand side.

4 Finish with a final piece of lace glued around the top of her knickers up to her waist (remember it was the era of big knickers).

Skirt

1 With right sides of the skirt facing, stitch around hem.

2 Clip curve of hem to stitch line in several places around the hem.

3 Stitch thin wire around the hemline. (I whipped the wire to the hem stitching.)

4 Carefully turn skirt right side out through the waist slit. (This is the fiddly part of the pattern.)

5 Straighten out the wire in the hemline, so that a nice curved hem is achieved. Press hem.

6 Slip skirt onto doll and then glue in place just under her bust line.

Bodice

1 Glue or stitch a piece of ribbon onto the doll's left front just below her breast (the raw edge will be covered later).

2 Take the ribbon up around her neck and give it a twist or two. (This gives a neater finish around the neck.)

3 Then take the ribbon down her right front to finish below her right breast.

4 Glue or stitch in place.

5 Finally, take another piece of ribbon around the doll's waist, turning under the raw edge at the back and glue, or stitch in place.

Finishing Touches

I wigged my 'Marilyn' in baby blonde curls and I glued flat-back crystals to her ears.

Suppliers

CaroDoug Miniatures
6 St Ethelbert Street
Hereford
HR1 2NR
Tel: +44 (0) 1432 267821
www.carodougminiatures.co.uk

Period miniature room settings and accessories

Dixie Collection
PO Box 575
Bromley
BR2 7WP
Tel: +44 (0) 20 84620700
www.dixiecollection.co.uk

Miniature haberdashery

Dylon
www.dylon.com

Fabric dyes, paints and pens

JLB Miniatures
80a Crayford High Street
Crayford
Kent
DA1 4EF
Tel: +44 (0) 1322 553325
E-mail:
llinos@jlbtrad.freeserve.co.uk

Lace, viscose wigging

Katy Sue Designs Ltd
Tedco Business Works
Henry Robson Way
South Shields
Tyne and Wear
NE33 1RF
Tel: +44 (0) 1914 274571
www.katysuedolls.com

Doll kits

Mini Mannequins
12 Middle Walk
Tunbridge Wells
Kent
TN2 3HH
Tel: +44 (0) 1892 521505
E-mail: janet.harmsworth@
blueyonder.co.uk

Doll kits, patterns and dressed dolls

Shepherd Miniatures
Customer Care
12 Freelands Rd
Cobham
Surrey
KT11 2ND
Tel: +44 (0) 1932 864239
www.shepherdminiatures.com

Miniature needlework equipment

Sue Jo's Enchanted Cottage
70 Wellburn Road
Donwell Village
Washington
Tyne & Wear
NE37 1DB
Tel: +44 (0) 1914 166411

Fabrics, lace, ribbon, rosettes, ribbon roses, needlework tools

Tee Pee Crafts
28 Holborn Drive
Mackworth
Derby
DE22 4DX
Tel: +44 (0) 1332 332772
www.teepeecrafts.co.uk

No-hole beads, glues, flat-back crystals and braid

The Dolls' House Draper
PO BOX 128
Lightcliffe
Halifax
West Yorkshire
HX3 8RN
Tel: +44 (0) 1422 201275

Cotton fabric, wigging, nylon netting, ribbon

The Silk Route
Cross Cottage
Cross Lane
Frimley Green
Surrey
GU16 6LN
Tel: +44 (0) 1252 835781

Selection of silk fabrics and threads

Warwick Miniatures
PO Box 1180
Leamington Spa
Warwickshire
CV33 9ZX
Tel: +44 (0) 1926 632330
www.warwickminiatures.com

Miniature ice skate blades

Contributors

Janet Harmsworth was taught to sew and embroider by her mother and grandmother. With this solid grounding, she went on to make many of her own clothes and it was inevitable that these skills would eventually couple with her fascination for historical costume and a childhood fascination with making dolls' clothes. She now runs the successful business Mini Mannequins, supplier of doll kits, patterns and dressed dolls.

Janet's projects can be found on pages: 10, 14, 22, 30, 36, 40, 44, 48, 52, 56, 62, 66, 70, 74, 80, 84, 88, 102, 106, 110, 114, 118, 122.

Carolyn Harding is one half of the CaroDoug Miniatures duo. Based in Hereford, they supply a variety of dolls' house wares and also work to commission. Previous hobbies of this creative team are making rag dolls and water colour painting. After discovering and becoming addicted to the world of miniatures, they took their hobby one step further and began producing items to sell. Their projects can be found in *The Dolls' House Magazine*.

Carolyn's projects can be found on pages 18 and 26.

Sue Johnson of Sue Jo's Enchanted Cottage developed an interest and love for art, embroidery and needlework from an early age. She has an enduring interest in ornate forms of dress such as bridal and evening wear. Her intricate skill and magical touch were soon noticed by *The Dolls' House Magazine,* for whom she regularly contributes. Sue is the author of *The Dolls' House Wedding Book* (GMC Publications, 2006).

Sue's projects can be found on pages 92 and 98.

Index

To request a full catalogue of GMC titles, please contact:

GMC Publications Ltd, Castle Place, 166 High Street, Lewes, East Sussex BN7 1XU, United Kingdom
Tel: 01273 488005 Fax: 01273 402866

www.gmcbooks.com